The Way *of the* Red Dragon

The Way of the Red Dragon

*Internal Alchemy,
Shamanic Power,
and the Journey Within*

John Myerson
and
Jay Thomas

© Copyright 2024: John G. Myerson and Jay Thomas
All rights reserved. No part of this book may be used or reproduced in any form or by any means, electronic or mechanical, including photocopying and recording, or by any information storage and retrieval system, without permission in writing from the authors.

First Edition 2024
Paperback ISBN: 978-0-9816420-2-4
EBook ISBN: 978-0-9816420-3-1

The Way of the Red Dragon:
Internal Alchemy, Shamanic Power, and the Journey Within
John Myerson and Jay Thomas

For inquiries:
LifeArts Press
WayoftheRedDragon.com

Front cover design by Eileen Clynes, exceptionalholiness.com

PLEASE NOTE:
The patient anecdotes in this book are real. Names and places have been changed to protect the identity, rights, and privacy of John Myerson's patients.

JOHN MYERSON DEDICATION

In memory of my mother
Harriette G. Myerson
November 1919–July 2017
May her memory be blessed

In memory of my dear Friend and Brother on the Way
Paul G. Gallagher
June 1944–March 2023
May we share more lifetimes together

JAY THOMAS DEDICATION

In memory of 'Fani'
Stephanus de Clercq
1963–2003
My first spirit guide in the Realms

Acknowledgements

First, I would like to thank all my teachers in this realm and others. I could not have made this journey without your help.

I would like to thank all my friends, patients, and fellow travelers along the Way for your support, kindness and commitment to bettering yourselves.

I want to especially thank co-author Jay Thomas. This was not an easy book for me to write. Jay kept me in line and focused over the four years it took us to complete this project. None of this could have been realized without his vision, writing skills, and support.

I would like to thank: John Shelton for your kindness in always being there when I needed help. Smitha Gollamudi for your support during cancer treatments. Ginnie Bonnici and Becky Resnick for your all your support and kindnesses. John DeMarco and Michael Short for staying with me through all the years of sword training. Christine Lee, Jessica Locke for all your healing work. My rehab trainers, Kirstin deFrees, Carol Nelson and Kevin

Wagner. Our readers Judith Robbins and Paul Rivenberg, Ben Hawes, Patty Gibbons and Heather Small. My men's group Andy, Paul and Peter, thirty-two years and still going strong.

Special thanks to our editor Audra Figgins who was wonderful to work with and to Eileen Clynes for designing the book cover.

Many thanks to our book writing guru Beth Frankl. This project was your idea and you kept us on track to stay true to the memoir structure.

To my wife/partner of fifty-one years, Laura Talmud. Without you, this book would not have happened. All my love.

Contents

Acknowledgements — vii
Foreword by Mike Short — xi
Introduction by Jay Thomas — xv
Preface — xxv

THE KOANS

1. Zen Journey — 3
2. Calling the Souls — 33
3. Sword of No Sword — 81
4. Threshhold Guardian — 123
5. Echoes in the Realms — 165

Afterword — 205
About the Authors — 209

Foreword

by Mike Short

I met John Myerson in 2010 at the suggestion of a colleague who thought we had some things in common: we had both gone to Harvard, started on a medical school track before becoming acupuncturists, had been athletes, and practiced martial arts. The rumor was that John was an impressive healer who treated extremely complex cases using shamanic techniques. He was also a natural fighter with the body of an NFL lineman who had turned to the internal arts decades earlier. I was deeply skeptical. I'd met teachers with similar biographies that hid shadow selves filled with anger, manipulation, addiction, and huge egos. But by all accounts, John was living a normal family life in the suburbs, and for fifty years he had been getting up every morning before 3 a.m. to meditate.

I remember a few things about our first meeting—how he turned at a particular angle so I could get through the door without him looming over me, his genuine laugh, and the conversation confirming some of our shared interests. He was easy to talk to.

I asked him questions. He gave simple but not easy answers. How do you treat someone with acupuncture? Put them in a state that promotes healing. How do you win a fight? Relax more than your opponent. How do you conquer fear? I don't remember what John said, but I suspected I would find an answer if I could spar with him.

A few weeks later, we met on his driveway in Wellesley, Massachusetts, with several of his long-term students. I had been studying Asian martial arts and wrestling for decades. The yearlong stint when I studied in Japan was immediately useful because I could sense the practice was not about fighting, in the same way that shodō (calligraphy) or ikebana (flower arranging) or chadō (tea ceremony) are not about brushes or flowers or tea.

Imagine crossing swords with someone who can physically overwhelm you in an instant. You move out of range, feeling with the tip of your sword. Your eyes are wide, and everything is moving quickly. But your sparring partner has been doing this for decades and meditates while you sleep. Every move you make becomes an opening for him. When you move in one direction, he is waiting. It is a repeating pattern, and then you realize your own thoughts and fears are creating these traps. Your sparring partner steadily rolls towards you like a wave, gradually breaking around you.

Crossing swords with John has a certain frisson. The blades are steel, and the feel is razor sharp and alive. It is unquestionably martial, but it is not about martial arts. The feeling is more like fielding a question from a Zen master that crystalizes or fragments your sense of self: the moment's intensity opens you. There is a sense of possibility if you stay in that space. This may be what John hints at when he tells his patients, "Be careful what you ask for because you will get an answer."

Over the years, students from many disciplines have been affected by their encounters with John and have become interested in his story. It is not because they are looking for motivation—working with him gives you just what you need. But it takes time to absorb the lessons, and it helps to learn about someone you trust who has worked at it for a lifetime. Although John is gregarious and approachable, he has always declined the role of guru, and when this happens, he quietly leaves the scene. This book is the natural byproduct of John's relentless path on behalf of others—and his path is unique. This is John's first lesson to his students: "I won't let you do it like me. You need to find your own way."

Michael Short, MAOM, Lic.Ac.
Assistant Professor
New England School of Acupuncture
Massachusetts College of Pharmacy and Health Sciences

Introduction

by Jay Thomas

Where would you expect to encounter a mystic, a healer, and a warrior shaman? Amid the tribes of the Amazon basin? In the mountains of Tibet? In the river valleys and forests of the Pacific Northwest? Indeed, I was surprised to find John Myerson in the suburbs of Boston in 2009. It seems the crossing of our paths was a gift for both of us to unwrap so we could each share, learn, and grow from our healing journeys. That's how I became the co-author of this book.

My story of healing is but one example of how John Myerson works with his patients and the significant impact of his unique style of present-day shamanism. John's access to the Realms is fluid and immediate. He slips seamlessly in and out of the Realms at any time and can include another in such an experience. That was the case with me.

I met John by chance. Or maybe it was destined. I was in pain—terrible emotional pain. As a librarian and avid reader, I searched for information about healing and any useful methods for getting clear of my distress. I had worked with psychotherapists and counselors since I was twenty years old. Still, at age forty-seven, pain consumed me. I was beleaguered by lingering heartache from childhood mistreatment—violence, neglect, abandonment. I was emotionally shut down and spiritually fractured. I was getting desperate, so much so I had selected a high bridge across the Connecticut River as a scenic conclusion to my life. I saw this as the probable release valve from my life-long anguish when I reached a point where I could no longer console my aching heart and tiring core. At the time, I was satisfied with this intention and plan.

Still grasping on to hope, I came across John's first book, *Riding the Spirit Wind: Stories of Shamanic Healing.* I was intrigued by John's credentials as a psychologist, acupuncturist, martial artist, and an accomplished Zen Master who was profoundly influenced by Taoism. And he was a modern shaman (whatever I understood that to be at the time). The book jacket indicated he lived in the next town over from me, a serendipitous coincidence. So, I sent him an email and told him my story, the saga of my broken self. I told him of the pain. I told him of the bridge. I was desperate. Whatever he might do had to work, because I had lost hope.

My first encounter with John was rather typical for any patient who meets with him. I know from first-hand accounts how his methods are effective and impactful. I interviewed more than twenty of John's patients during our first phase of structuring this book to get those narratives.

We met in his Framingham office. That day, I wondered where the feathers were. *Isn't he going to smudge me or bless me or something?* I thought. I saw a bell sitting on a table next to him. *Maybe he'll ring it? Isn't that how shamans open ceremonies?* I would soon find out how unique this man was. Like other psychotherapists, he listened to my litany of sorrow and despair. Unlike others, he went somewhere else—the Realms—assessing energy and looking for any hindrances. And then he did something even more remarkable: he invited me into that mystical space with him.

He took me to a river, a place where I always felt at peace and connected. John was present. He was there, inside my vision, with me in my waking dreamscape. But he wasn't visible. Yet I could sense his presence in this river realm while I heard his instructions, some concise verbal cues spoken a few feet across the room from where he was seated.

He coaxed me to feel the energy of the current of the water, to welcome and accept the flow.

"Just be with it." He said.

But this flow, this current, was much more than a movie I got dropped into, more than what seemed like a virtual reality, high-definition dreamscape.

It was numinous. Metaphysical. And transcendent.

John continued, "This is a place of Power for you."

'Huh' I thought. *'What kind of person speaks about Power?' 'And what exactly does that mean?'*

I could sense he brought me there to appease my emotional turbulence, which it did. It anchored me. Yes, I was soothed. Very much so. But there was something else beyond my five senses, something conceptual or maybe even ideological. He wanted to show me that change is possible. It was a lesson in the agency of healing through internal alchemy—that profound change is my responsibility and can be had on my own terms and in my own way.

I knew from that point forward—if I rose to the challenge—I'd have to loosen and lose my story, an epic story as the victim.

That narrative held an identity I had shaped, nurtured, and defended my whole life. Somehow, I knew the journey within would not be an easy one, but well worth it.

John continued: "I don't know if I can heal you."

I gasped.

He then said, "Maybe I could. But I won't."

I was aghast. I could feel my brow furrow.

"I can teach you how to heal yourself." John said while gazing intently into my eyes.

I was crestfallen.

Admittedly, I was disappointed as I understood part of his intention: he won't cure me. The truth is, he never offered to.

Instead, he gifted me the hope I needed at the time—his intention and commitment to work with me. He was open to being my guide, to leading me through healing myself by giving me the tools to do so, by teaching me how and modelling the skills for me. Moreover, he told me he'd help me and show me how to heal myself.

I was perplexed. That's not what I expected to hear.

I really wanted him to do some mystical woo and, in a few sessions, take away my pain.

"Isn't that what shamans do?!" I asked myself.

That first encounter began a cascade of true healing, showing me how to transmute my suffering through many techniques. Quieting my mind. Releasing anger. Resolving decades of heartache. Exploring and deepening compassion for myself and others. Caring for my body. Cleansing my psyche. Reconnecting to my repressed and suppressed emotions. Awakening my Soul. Letting go of the stories that no longer served me. Living my truth. Finding my Power. I attribute my integration to the steady love and guidance of my teacher and his practice of shamanic healing—with and for me—through both gentle and tough love, always with the resolute grit of his warrior spirit.

John has modelled for me all the principles he talks about in this book. He has taken me to the Realms, those indefinable spaces/places of non-ordinary reality. He has Called the Souls for me and with me, those energetic entities often needed to do shamanic workings. He helped me heal my dark, heavy emotional states of anger and sadness by using loving energy as the tool for transmutation.

John helped me understand Power as condensed energy for healing as he seamlessly slips between consensus reality and The Realms to gather information and for connecting with Spirit. The ineffable energy that binds us all together? John calls that dynamic force the One which has a myriad of descriptive names such as God, the Holy Spirit, Great Spirit, the Tao, and many other words that fall short of its true understanding and transcendent experience.

Most notable, to me, is Radical Freedom, a teaching technique John uses with all his patients. In this paradigm there are no forms, no formal guidance, no required learning to be assessed. Rather, a 'student' is expected to come up with their own objectives and methods of learning. What's the best way to discover and integrate knowledge and experience? By connecting to what we know, to what resonates for us and then expanding our skills, in our own time, to achieve our set intentions. This is a model for the inspired and self-motivated. Surely, John gives guidance. Yet he believes everyone learns at a different rate and we each have our own ways of seeing, feeling, and knowing—and of making meaning in our lives. Therefore, each of his patients is kindly and mindfully tended to. Often that includes koans, riddles without answers. They are used in Zen Buddhism as one way of puzzling out internal blocks and ultimately helping us etch pathways for connecting with the One.

Accessing the Realms, Calling the Souls, teaching about Power, the Way, the One, Transmutation, Radical Freedom, and Koans: these are signature concepts that John uses with all his patients, sometimes overtly, sometimes not so explicitly. You will encounter these terms and concepts throughout this book.

In December of 2020, the vaccines for Covid had just rolled out. Time felt more fluid while much of the world stopped or in an unprecedented manner continued online. That is when, through a Zoom meeting, John asked me to help him with this project. Immediately I asked him, "What will be distinct in this work from your prior three books?" John told me he wanted to chronicle his life story. He was finally ready to be vulnerable, exposing the backstories which he had not yet shared before. Little did he know that we would embark upon a four-year journey of unravelling some of his potent unresolved matters—the koans of his life.

The book served as a catalyst for me, too. I was "that guy," one of John's patients who relentlessly asked him just how he does it. I wanted to know the ins and outs of his shamanic practices. I needled him often for information and for clarity. With his ability to access the Realms and his energetic skills, I wanted to know why... I asked, "John, why can't you heal yourself from your own physical maladies?" Adeptly, John retorted, "It's not a question of *why or why not*, Jay, rather it's a question of *how to*." Within this inquisitive framework, we shared hundreds and hundreds of hours of discussion while sorting through many of those defining anecdotes which have shaped his life as a healer. It has made for a fascinating account; one he has not revealed until now.

In this book, readers will learn about John's truly extraordinary story—one that molded him into the enigmatic archetypes he exemplifies as mystic, healer, warrior, and shaman. The combined grit of these personas is what makes him a fierce warrior shaman. Initially, we named each section a chapter. Then, John realized he was describing his own koans, his own life riddles that needed resolution:

Koan 1: Zen Journey, tells the story of John's Zen Buddhist training in the Zendo.

Koan 2: Calling the Souls, recounts how John met his shamanic teacher and how he unexpectedly trained in accessing the Realms and working within them.

Koan 3: Sword of No Sword, relates John's life-long martial arts training and the honing of his Warrior archetype, with an unexpected shamanic overlay.

Koan 4: Threshold Guardian, describes a pivotal shift in John's Power, as he came to terms with his own inner strength, his warrior archetype, and his own intrinsic resistance.

Koan 5: Echoes in the Realms, reveals the important interaction—and healing power—of non-ordinary reality, as John encountered inexplicable and peculiar events that helped resolve a long-standing, puzzling mystery.

John sees these koans as periods of his life wherein he claimed two hard fought prizes: integration and resolution. Together, the stories of Koans 1 through 4 describe how John resolved his first life koan: he integrated his four primary archetypes: mystic, healer, warrior, and shaman. Koan 5, by itself, describes how John resolved his second life koan: the lifelong quest for understanding a mysterious and harrowing childhood vision of the Holocaust that became more complex and more distressing throughout the decades.

Since the sections/koans have been assembled thematically, some of the narratives are nonlinear in that they actually span years or even decades of John's lifetime. Also, because John slips between ordinary and non-ordinary reality (the Realms), he often found it difficult to pinpoint exactly when an event took place. We did our best to recreate the scenarios and details from those memories of long ago.

John's life story is epic. It is a tale of remarkable strength and resilience. I am one of many hundreds of people over many decades for whom John has helped. He brings about healing and wellness through Internal Alchemy, Shamanic Power, and the Journey Within. Internal Alchemy refers to the transmutation of energy, often from darkness to light. Power is condensed energy. Used with shamanic practices, this Power is for healing. The Journey Within is introspective. It helps us get clear of emotional and psycho-spiritual static, anything that keeps us from connecting to the One. Those three elements, contained in the subtitle of this book— *Internal Alchemy, Shamanic Power, and the Journey Within*—truly are the modes John uses for transformation both for himself and for all of his patients. Undoubtedly, he embodies these principles with integrity: it is his Way (one he calls *The Way of the Red Dragon*). No smudging. No feathers. No bells. John gets to the heart of the matter without fanfare. His Zen leanings are always apparent. He talks the talk and he walks the walk. He exemplifies the Mahayana Boddhisattva ideal by making an offering of his life for the healing of humanity. His impact on the lives of others is extensive and significant.

Weekly, I drive through Western Massachusetts over that picturesque bridge that might have been the scene of my own tragedy. That crossing over the Connecticut River for me is both heartrending and joyful. The span itself is an apt metaphor for healing and human potential: traversing such a chasm is possible—one can safely get to the other side with the right guidance and support. John Myerson has provided me—and so many others—those life-affirming gifts.

I'm confident the stories in this book will both inspire and amaze you.

Jay Thomas, M.A., M.Ed.

Preface

This is a book about Power.

Defining Power has always been somewhat elusive to me, because from a shamanic perspective, it is ineffable. It is not something one reads about and then understands. Power is experienced. Power is cultivated. Power is honed over time. It is complex. It is nuanced. Yet, we need words as a bridge to understanding.

When my patients ask me to define Power, I first make the distinction of Power over versus Power within. Power over is driven by ego and fear. Power within is connected to the One and to the cooperative human spirit, of inspired and caring expressions.

Power is a form of energy. Power, as condensed energy, can be used or directed as one decides—or is called to use it. People can plug into their natural sources of energy—using mind, body, and spirit—to drive their talents, interests, and abilities. Typically, most folks get stuck in fear. When they block their natural connection to the One, they hamper the flow of their Power. Usually, it takes many years to get clear enough to reclaim it. This is the challenging undertaking and commitment of psychotherapists and spiritual counselors—to help folks identify and resolve any obstacles to self-knowledge.

My clients often ask me, "Where do you get your Power from?" The simple answer is, "The One." More concisely, I would say, "Through expressions of the One." My mentors and teachers helped me find my Power by offering me their structures. I used what I learned from them as a template. I felt free to shape their offerings as needed. I honed my skills for my own personal growth and to work with my patients in my healing practice.

The ensuing chapters of this book explore thematically how I was introduced to—and wrangled with—Power. It was a nonlinear journey, as most expeditions often are. My journey both for claiming and expressing my Power was at times arduous and mostly undefined. It wasn't until I partnered with my coauthor, Jay Thomas, to write this book that I discovered five clear motifs which influenced my life calling—Zen immersion, shamanic training, Taoist and martial arts studies, warrior archetype, and working in the Realms. These were five significant koans—riddle-like challenges that can only be solved through life experience. These koans are themes which capture important threads of how I have used Power, woven throughout the tapestry of my lifespan.

The Way of the Red Dragon is my story. It tells of how I cultivated Shamanic Power. It gives examples of how the only way out of psychospiritual and emotional turmoil is through. For myself, and for my patients, resolution comes by embracing Inner Alchemy and the Journey Within. Surely, that inner passage of excavation and revelation is easier said than done.

The Way is more than just a path for me. It is from the *Tao Te Ching* by Lao Tzu (sixth century BCE), which roughly translates as "The Way of Power," known by Taoists as the inherent order of the Universe, the Way of Nature, of "action without action." Simply put, it's going with the flow, an important lesson I keep relearning with each life challenge. How so? By making myself vulnerable. I open my heart chakra and extend my energy as a bridge to the One.

Cultivating Power has been a lifelong quest and theme for me. Writing this book helped me further explore how that pursuit has influenced my personal development as a contemporary healer. The writing naturally evolved because I knew I was merely the conduit for Spirit to engage. I did not make a definitive plan of action, yet I did set the stage for possibilities to unfold. I learned to trust my instincts in "ordinary reality," which for me is to be in the moment and allow for the natural flow, just as I do in "non-ordinary reality" with shamanic workings. That's what I call *applied Zen*, perhaps with a mystical application. Most importantly, I learned to trust the Souls. They are the stewards and guides. I am in service to them. I allowed myself to be informed by them and yield to the creative process. It is how I have lived my life, as the Red Dragon, a moniker I took in the 1970s and carried forward through my Taoist studies.

"Where's the Power?" I ask this question often when assessing people and situations. I suppose the real question for you as the reader of this book is, "Where's *your* Power?" Initially, the answer harkens back to an inventory of emotional defense mechanisms and the ways we disconnect from our Selves and the One through ego attachments and the tangle of interpersonal situations. To me, that's psychology 101. That is, how do we give up our Power? And why? Reclaiming our Power is a process and a commitment. Such a journey is not for the faint of heart because discovery and recovery is messy. "Where's the Power?" Without hesitation, I point to you. It is within you. It is within all of us. I strive to help my patients discern and reclaim self-empowerment. If they can identify their own energy patterns and the energy patterns of others, they can realize and nurture their own Power in the world.

Cultivating Power is layered, like the complexity of a tree, where deep and expansive roots are needed to nurture the growth of a solid trunk for branches to extend out and above to finer expressions. A robust, rugged tree is time-tested, taking years to mature, enduring the challenges of many seasons of growth.

Some people call me a shaman. I think of myself as a mystic. To me a mystic is someone who wants a direct experience of the One. While a shaman does things in the Realms, like healing, I'm called to do both.

Some people say that I am a warrior. I know I am. It is my archetype. It is how I am in the world. Yet, I think of myself as a healer, too, a healer who uses and directs Power. As such, when working in the Realms both with darkness and the light, I am a warrior shaman.

Mystic. Shaman. Warrior. Healer. I combined these four roles and attributes. Sometimes I am a warrior shaman, sometimes a shamanic healer. Sometimes I'm a mystic shaman. I always direct energy for healing when Power is flowing through me. Ultimately, the Power is not yours. It is not mine. It comes from the One. It flows through me. It flows through you. It flows through us all—if we are unencumbered and allow it.I hope my story and the contents of this book inspires you to find your own Power.

John Myerson
June, Full Buck Moon
2024: The Year of the Dragon
LT Farm
Dover, Massachusetts

The Way *of the* Red Dragon

KOAN 1

I never wore robes. Others did. People were sitting in the meditation space, downstairs in the Victorian house that served as the Zendo. At one time it was the living room. In the next room—what used to be the dining room—more than a dozen were seated on the floor, on their cushions. I was meditating, looking at the wall. Three feet in front of me was beige painted drywall. A person to the left. Another to the right. No movement. No sound. Stillness. Quiet. Until I heard a bell.

I was next.

I stood up and walked up the stairs to what had been a bedroom. Now, it was the dokusan room.

I could feel the tension.

I asked myself, Do I have the answer? Can I stay there with her? Can I connect?

I thought, Maybe. Maybe this time. . . .

Zen Journey

I began studying martial arts when I was fifteen, the kind of martial arts that originated in the Shaolin Buddhist temple in China. The monks needed guards to protect the temple from raiders, so they learned techniques introduced by the Bodhidharma, an Indian monk who brought Chan Buddhism from India to China (c. 500 CE). When Chan Buddhism moved to Japan, it was then called Zen.

In my sophomore year in college, 1971, I became interested in Buddhism. I asked one of my roommates to recommend some books to me. There were six of us in a suite, in Adams house, near Harvard Square. The other dorms were located down the street along the banks of the Charles River. We would practice our Kung Fu forms on the grassy area of the riverbank. I was studying ancient Chinese history at the time, yet I really didn't really know much about Buddhism.

I asked my roommate, "What is distinct about the Shaolin monks?"

He didn't know. Yet I was on a quest to find out more. I later learned from my reading Shaolin monks may enter the monastery as young as the age of three. They train how to control *chi* (energy) through meditation. It takes a lot of discipline and awareness to embody this concept.

I knew the monks studied Zen—and lived it—but I really didn't understand it. What did it mean to "live Zen?" *Zen* is the Japanese pronunciation of the Chinese word *chan*, which comes from a Sanskrit root meaning "thought," "absorption," or "meditation." Some scholars believe chan developed from the interaction between Mahayana Buddhism and Taoism.

Then, I asked him, "Can you recommend some books about Zen?"

He suggested a few, including *The Three Pillars of Zen: Teaching, Practice, and Enlightenment* by Roshi Philip Kapleau, one of the first American-born Zen Masters. As soon as I could, I headed out to the cozy bookstore around the corner at Bow and Mt. Auburn Streets in Cambridge, Massachusetts. The Grateful Union Bookstore was located just across the way from the dorm. I bought the book and quickly read it. I thought to myself, *Oh my God, there are people out there who think like I do.* I was so excited.

On the book jacket I saw the author lived in Rochester, New York. He hosted several weekends each year where beginners could come and meditate for a day at his retreat center. I really wanted to meet him, so I organized a group of friends and off we went. Kapleau had converted an old house into a *Zendo*—a place where people gather to practice Zen Buddhism, much like a church or a temple.

We were greeted at the door by monks wearing formal robes with shaved heads. To me, it was exotic. I was intrigued. Also, it was foreign to me because I had never experienced anything like it. We were told to take our shoes off and the monks then gave us lots of additional instructions, which included how to sit—that is, how to meditate. As the day went on the monks continued with more directives. *So many edicts*, I thought. It seemed like Kapleau was bringing the strictures of traditional Japan to Rochester.

This was my first Zen experience replete with ceremony. At home, I would sit quietly, in the dorm room on the floor, either with my legs crossed (*siddhasana*) or in a kneeling position (*seiza*). I must admit, at first sitting was brutally difficult because it was a challenge to empty my active, busy mind. However, I could sit for twenty minutes without much difficulty. When I could, I would sit alone outside on park benches or on the grass under a tree.

In this Zendo, I experienced formal sitting. We all sat facing the wall, each with our cushions on the floor. We were instructed to sit perfectly straight, our hands in universal mudra: left hand on top of right with the thumbs touching. Our eyes were open in soft gaze directed toward a spot three feet in front of us. The tongue was to be touching the upper palate behind the teeth. No movement was allowed—no chatter, no noise. All commands were given by ringing bells. We sat for some time and then walked slowly in a line. Then we repeated this cycle three times.

Eventually, Kapleau spoke to the group. He was in his late fifties or sixties, though it was hard to tell because his head was shaved, like the other monks. He had a stern disposition. I heard the words "commitment" and "dedication" and even more about "rules" on how to do just about everything. It didn't feel right to me. I felt boxed in.

After lunch, we each got to meet with Kapleau individually for a brief encounter. I was thrilled to meet the head of the Zendo—the *roshi* (teacher) was an honored person. Yet, this was not a dialogue. He spoke *at* me. He said, "You should leave college and come and be a monk. Everything else is a waste of time, including martial arts. You will not get anywhere without a teacher."

He dismissed me, as one does to a minion. I left feeling shocked, numb, and disoriented. This was not how I imagined this situation would unfold. Immediately, I didn't like him. He was dogmatic and to me, a zealot. We did not connect at all. *Where was the compassion? Isn't that what Buddhism is about?* I asked myself.

Yet, this was the first experience I had formally sitting with a group under the guidance of a Zen Master. It was disappointing. This was all new to me. Since I had never been to a monastery, I was surprised there were strict rules on how to do just about everything. There was no freedom, per se. I know myself: I thrive in environments that encourage autonomy, and I leave situations where I feel ensnared in conventions. I felt so trapped, though I did connect easily to the quiet sitting, probably because I was used to sitting by myself silently. I liked letting my mind float out and away from me. I didn't know it at the time, but this practice would give me access to the Realms for my future shamanic work.

Nonetheless, Kapleau's book uncovered some important distinctions for me, namely Soto versus Rinzai Zen. These are the two sects of Zen practiced in the United States. The practice of Zen meditation is called *zazen*. In meditation, Rinzai Zen uses *koans*, which are succinct, paradoxical statements or questions that have no answer. Soto Zen mainly uses *shikantaza*, which means "just sitting." I've experienced five approaches of shikantaza: focused concentration on a point, soft focus gazing at a vista, following the breath, mantra (sound), and mandala (visualization).

From reading Kapleau's book, I was mostly intrigued by the concept of satori. *Satori* (also called *kensho*) means the experience of "awakening," an expansion of consciousness, which for a brief moment connects us directly to the One. Such an experience mostly cannot be expressed in words because it is a form of transcendence. To me, the enlightenment experience is just one gateway for connecting with the One. At the time, I really wanted this. It became a hunger for me. I was yearning for it—satori, awakening, enlightenment, kensho (whatever you call it)—even though I didn't know exactly what that meant.

When I returned to Cambridge, I sought out various informal meditation groups. I tried a Korean Zen center where I bought my first meditation cushion. Also, I sat with a couple of newly formed Tibetan groups, but they were more focused on lectures. Talks didn't interest me. I attended other small gatherings with people who just wanted to meditate together in their living rooms.

For the next few years, I sat with my dear friend, "Elder Brother" and Taoist teacher, Paul Gallagher. I enjoyed our Taoist meditations because they were unique from the focused Zen practice of just following the breath or shikantaza. With shikantaza, our attention is neither narrow nor diffuse, neither one-pointed nor distracted. We are completely present with each thought, feeling, and sensation, watching it arise and pass away in our minds. In effect, we neither "do" nor "not do."

Sometimes we set intentions to move energy; for example, we would practice Inner Heavenly Circulation or Microcosmic Orbit. In these, we would bring the chi up the spine with each inhalation and then down the front of the body with each exhalation. We also practiced the Golden Light Meditation, where we would imagine a small light in our heart center and then slowly expand the light until it encompassed the heart. Then we would expand the light until it included the entire chest, followed by the entire body, and eventually magnifying the intention to include the Universe.

Eight years after my encounter with Kapleau at his Zendo in Rochester, I was dedicated and consistent in my meditation practice, sitting from thirty to sixty minutes each day, totaling thousands of hours. Because Paul was a scholar of Taoist Cultivation, he was attuned to the local activities of the Taoist/Buddhist community. Somehow, he learned about Maurine Stuart, the roshi at the Cambridge Buddhist Association on Sparks Street. Paul knew of my interest in Zen, so he suggested that I check out the Zendo with him. We attended a Sunday morning sit that Maurine led. It lasted three hours. I think Zen felt too formal for Paul, yet I loved it and wanted more.

I had an instant connection with Maurine. She had a way of looking deep inside of me. Her eyes would keenly focus on me—just me. I could sense her profound compassion emanating from her whole being and projecting out through her eyes. She looked beyond the exterior and into my being. Her voice wasn't loud, yet it was penetrating in that it resonated with Power. I had never experienced that before. I felt like I had come home.

I did not return to the Zendo for a few months. In February of 1979, just as I arrived, Maurine was pulling into the driveway. She got out of her car, caught my gaze, and said, "Hi John, I always knew I would see you again." There was something auspicious about our encounter. The eight years to come would draw me deeper into clearing my mind and singularly focusing on the present moment. I was open to pushing myself beyond my current abilities. I thought, *This may be an opportunity to do so.*

I was intrigued, both by Maurine and the Zendo. Inside the Zendo, there was no orientation, per se. This is classic form with the Japanese—no formal instructions, you just got to figure it all out based on the context. We were shown the standing bow, a respectful stance upon entering the meditation room. I was directed to a cushion and told to sit up straight with my legs crossed and face the wall. Unlike my experience with Kapleau in New York, this Zendo was rather casual. I never wore robes, though others did. We could wear whatever we wanted—sweatpants, long pants, and t-shirts were fine as long as the colors were not too loud and distracting.

There were some formalities, such as bells used to mark time and bowing when leaving the meditation room, but for the most part the principal focus was on the sitting rather than rules and decorum. The large rectangular-shaped meditation room, formerly a living room of this Victorian house, had big square pillows, called *zabutons*, on the floor, lined up along the wall. Typically, they were very close to each other with little separation, like seats in a theater. Atop the zabutons were *zafus*, round cushions to sit on. The zabutons cushioned our legs while the zafus provided a seat.

Each of us silently filed into the room, found our space, and waited for the roshi—Maurine—to enter. There really was no anticipation for me; once I was on my cushion, I settled in swiftly by finding my breath, using each inhale and exhale as a calming wave. When Maurine arrived, she positioned herself at the head of the room, next to a fireplace. Then, Maurine rang a large, hammered metal bell positioned in front of her. It was impressive in size, perhaps three feet high and about a foot-and-a-half wide. Three strikes on the bell with a wooden clapper broke the silence, signaling the start of the session. The antique brass echoed through the room its solemn, deep resonant timbre. This session lasted three hours: fifty minutes of sitting followed by ten minutes of walking. We repeated this three times over.

After the session was done, people filed out quietly. Talking was permitted outside of the meditation room in the front hall where we put our coats and shoes. I am not sure what else happened because I left right away. I was not there for social reasons. I was seeking something profound, although I wasn't exactly sure what that was. Yet, I knew it was there in the Zendo—and Maurine was the key.

Maurine was an intriguing, complex person. At the Zendo, she was omnipresent. As the Zen Master and Roshi, Maurine was completely in charge. She was the director of all the programming, she managed all the people including her primary assistant and the live-in students/caretakers, she performed the training and supervision of the priests, and took care of the integration of the laypeople who visited and frequented the trainings. Maurine was the spiritual backbone of the Zendo, overseeing all operations and providing spiritual counseling and direction, including priestly duties such as officiating at weddings and funerals.

Maurine was born in the Canadian prairies and grew up in a small village in Keeler, Saskatchewan. She was a talented pianist who studied music at the University of Manitoba. After she graduated, she was awarded a grant to study in music in France. It was in Paris she discovered books on Buddhism, especially Zen. She then moved to New York City where she met her husband and raised three children. In New York, she encountered her first Zen teacher, Shimano Eido Roshi. He was Japanese born, trained in Rinzai Zen, and the Zen Master at the Zen Studies Society located in Manhattan. Maurine's family then moved to Boston for her husband's business. In Boston, she met people who ran the Cambridge Buddhist Association (CBA) where D.T. Suzuki—a famous Japanese professor who taught at Harvard and is attributed with bringing Zen to America—was president. After Suzuki retired, Maurine was invited to come and teach at CBA.

None of this really mattered to me. I was drawn to the experience of Zen, not the accolades and backstories. Yet, there was something unique about Maurine. I went to the Zendo every Sunday morning for the three-hour sessions. I was driven to deepen my practice, as the structure of the Zendo under the guidance of Maurine resonated for me. To me, the character of the teacher and the vibe of the *sangha* (community) mattered more than the lineage. I showed up when it fit into my hectic schedule. I didn't attend during the week because I had my family to care for—I was married with three children under the age of five. Also, I was working full-time with my Oriental medicine and psychotherapy practices.

The routine at the Zen Center was repeated meditation. It is the fundamental practice for the sangha. Regularly, there were extended meditation sessions, called *sesshin*. This period was distinct because it lasted five to eight days. *Sesshin* literally means "touching the heart-mind." Such focus can bring one's mind to a heightened awareness. The community would devote themselves almost exclusively to Zen meditation practice—twelve to sixteen hours daily. Maurine was flexible, allowing anyone to participate in any time block. This was unique because in other Zendos the sesshin was restricted in that people had to commit to the entire event.

The sesshin had a unique feature—*dokusan*—which translates from English to Japanese as "go alone." In Rinzai Zen, dokusan refers to meeting one-on-one with the Zen Master. It is not a discussion. It is more of an encounter. But the encounter is designed to stir one's equilibrium, to push students into a spiritual crisis.

Those wanting to meet with Maurine waited in a separate room from the rest of the sangha. Each time, we would all sit on our zabutons facing the wall meditating. At first, I felt anxious because this process could take hours. We each waited—and meditated—until it was our specific time. I knew I was next when the cushion beside me became vacant and I heard a beckoning bell ringing from the upstairs landing.

Unlike the others who solemnly ascended the stairs, I hurried up them. I was eager. The dokusan room was on the right side of the second floor. It was a cozy space, perhaps ten feet by ten feet, just enough room for two people. I entered. I fully prostrated three times; that is, I kneeled, sliding my body outward until my stomach met the floor with my legs and arms extended and my hands stretched beyond my head. Then I rose to standing and bowed three times from the waist with my hands in *gassho*, the Japanese gesture of bringing the hands together in front of the heart. This rite honors the Three Pillars of Buddhism: Buddha, Dharma, Sangha.

Finally, after all this ceremony, I sat on the cushion. Maurine sat an arm's length in front of me on her cushion. She looked at me—and into me. Those eyes, those penetrating eyes! There was no time to collect my thoughts. Each encounter would be different. Sometimes she would say, softly, "Yes?" Sometimes she said nothing. Her gaze could last seconds or minutes. I never knew for how long because time was fluid in that space.

Aside from the protocols of the greeting and parting, there were no rules. Anything could happen. This is the way with dokusan, everywhere, worldwide. Some teachers yell or strike their students with a stick, not to harm but to surprise. With me, Maurine was gentle. She might give a few words of encouragement or just sit quietly peering at me intensely. I could feel her Power. It was solid. And lovely. Still, each time I was both excited and anxious. I wanted to connect to her Power because each meeting was an opportunity—the gateway—to satori.

Mostly, Maurine didn't ask me questions during dokusan. I'm not sure why, except that I knew the true intention was not a verbal transmission of knowledge but an energy exchange. Each time, Maurine was making some determination about me. She was deciding something in that exact moment, during that "interview" and "non-conversation." And then my bubble was broken—she rang the bell. I rose to my feet, executed the three full prostrations followed by three bows. Away I went. Out the door. Down the stairs. Back on my cushion.

This was the routine for the next seven years.

At times, I would receive a koan from Maurine. These riddles are puzzles, brainteasers of sorts, given for the student "solve." Maurine expected me to sort out this problem and present her with an "answer." Moreover, there are no hints or instructions on what to do with the koan, following the Japanese tradition whereby no one tells you the rules or protocols. Since the koan has no actual solution or right answer, its intention is to create a mind crisis. Koans entrap the mind, I discovered. When you get caught in this place enough times, you release. The mind stops its usual chatter, and you step over the threshold the ego has set up to keep you in your habitual, self-limiting mind. The result: you let go.

I remember the first koan Maurine gave me, a classic one that is formally called Chao-chou's Dog: *A monk asked Master Chao-chou, "Has a dog the Buddha Nature or not?" Chao-chou said, "Mu!"*

Mu means "no." No doubt, I was confused.

There are other groups who practice meditation-like koans with the intention to fill the conscious mind with so much information that you let go when you become intellectually overwhelmed. For example, some religious scholars and serious-minded disciples contentiously debate their holy texts, including ultra-orthodox Jews, Tibetan Buddhists, and those in Korean Zen sects. U.S. Marines and the Japanese Yamabushu monks push limits of the mind through the body with rigorous training by driving recruits to the point of "seizing" the body/mind. Japanese marathon monks do similar, alternating a rigorous cycle of running and *taiko* drumming.

Outside of the Zendo, I applied the koan model to my martial arts training with the sword. To me, Zen is sword, sword is Zen. This can be traced back to Zen Buddhism as the religion of the samurai. As skilled swordsmen, samurai warriors had to command total focus if they were to be successful on the battlefield. Also in Japan, the shogun, as the head of the military, was a sword practitioner. He was a disciple of Zen and used the important principle of *mushin* (no mind), the art of both having an empty mind and also seeing everything around him at the same time. The mental state of mushin is necessary for solving koans (which I also use when entering the Realms with the sword).

For the most part, sesshins were scheduled to take place monthly. The format was the same every day. I always took the opportunity to experience dokusan. I looked forward to it. I loved the challenge. I treasured meeting with Maurine one on one.

Each time was the same and different because the experience was unpredictable.

At each sesshin, I would meditate, looking three feet in front of me to the beige painted plaster wall. A person to the left. Another to the right. No movement. No sound. Stillness. Quiet. Until I heard a bell.

I was next.

I stood up and walked up the stairs to the dokusan room.

I could feel the tension.

I asked myself, *Do I have the answer? Can I stay there with her? Can I connect?*

I thought, *Maybe. Maybe this time....*

My experience with Maurine was a combination of using koans and shikantaza. In the beginning, I found koans challenging. As time progressed, during dokusan Maurine and I mostly sat together. In essence, we shared the experience of shikantaza without koans. This became a mind-to-mind practice. I connected to her. She read me. I can't really describe where we went together—it was somewhere or someplace in the Realms.

Over the years my meditation practice deepened. I felt less aggressive, more peaceful internally. I was able to focus better. My mind was clearer. That is the key intention for practicing Zen—clearing the mind. Surely, I think my ability to focus was enhanced as I developed a heightened awareness that included honing my sense of seeing and feeling and my own direct connection to the One. My consciousness was expanding, ultimately increasing my awareness of the One.

During one sesshin, I finally felt my mind was clear for the whole three hours of the meditation period. When it was time for dokusan, I was excited. I wanted to show Maurine how I had improved.

I sat and waited for an hour or more until it was my turn. I heard the bell, jumped from my cushion, and ran up the stairs to the dokusan room. In the hallway just outside of the room, I bowed to the person who had just seen Maurine.

I entered, completed my bows, got onto the cushion, and looked into Maurine's eyes. As usual, she was three feet in front of me.

"I did it!" I blurted out. "I cleared my mind!"

Clearly, I had lost my concentration. Obviously, she did not see it. She looked at me as though I were a nut cake from the hospital down the street. In fact, her expression was one of concern that I had lost my mind—and not in a Zen way!

I felt like a blithering idiot.

Maurine reached for the bell and rang it.

It was less than fifteen seconds. Dismissed. I was done.

I performed the required bows. I left the dokusan room.

As I walked down the stairs, I lost my composure and laughed at myself.

Instead of going back into the Zendo to continue meditating, I had to go into the backyard to calm down.

So it goes.

The dokusan process is an essential part of Zen training. In essence, it was an assessment. After each unsuccessful "answer," the tension builds. I wasn't wrong, per se. I just was not connecting to her and the One. Maurine was not judging me. Rather, she was holding a mirror to myself so I could see where I needed to improve. That was my challenge moving forward.

Maurine gave *dharma* talks—the teachings of the Buddha—every day at sesshins. They could be just a few minutes long or up to twenty minutes or so. These were her interpretations of the original texts of the Buddha. Admittedly, I didn't listen to them.

Rather, I was meditating while she spoke. I didn't see the value of these talks in helping me attain a mind-to-mind connection with Maurine. As a mystic, I wanted to connect to the One, not engage in intellectual exercises. These stories just diverted my attention to theories and reflections.

Sometimes I asked myself, *Why am I putting so much time into this training?* If there were all kinds of people dynamics with politics and hierarchies to maneuver, I would have left the Zendo in a moment. But the only hurdles were in my mind.

It took me several years to have my first satori experience:

I complete my bows, get onto the cushion in the dokusan room, and look into Maurine's eyes. I notice the energy of the room has changed. It is heightened. And alive. I feel the room vibrating and humming.

It is a beautiful February day. Very cold and clear. Frost on the windows, the blue sky behind Maurine's head as she looks at me— and into me.

This moment. Something in me clicks.

I feel a huge shift in my perception of my world. The world both inside and outside of me changes.

Those eyes. She looks beyond my exterior and into my being.

Power. I feel her Power. Lots of Power.

I let her in. I let go. Wholly.

For the first time ever, I surrender my being to another.

She and I merge.

We become one. No boundary between us.

This is it—the mind-to-mind transmission.

My mind becomes so clear—mushin.

How much time passes? I don't know. We are outside of ordinary reality. It could be seconds. Or minutes.

Back into the room. But not totally back.

Am I really back?
I am different.
She smiles at me.

Looking back after several decades, I can better understand what Maurine was doing during dokusan. She was holding space for me. She would open a portal—an energetic space—and wait for me to join her there. This is the essence of the mind-to-mind transmission. I "solved" the koan by joining her. This was only the beginning. Maurine then used additional koans or meditations to deepen the experience.

To me, Zen is a use-it-or-lose-it practice. I have found I must keep the connection active. In essence, as a dedicated student, I see it is my responsibility to keep that space/portal open with my teacher. Eventually, I learned to go there by myself and reproduce this state of mind in my own practice, outside of the Zendo. That's when Maurine stopped using koans with me.

The intention of Zen training with the roshi is to attain enlightenment. I really don't like that word because it construes a one-time peak experience of mystical expanded awareness. I believe one deepens one's practice and continues to grow after that achievement. To me, there is no finish line, per se. There is no single summit because there are plenty of other mountains to climb. There is always room for improvement.

Traditionally, dharma transmission is when the roshi feels the student has learned all of the Buddha's teaching. This is much more than reading, learning, and reciting the *sutras* (the written teachings of the Buddha). It is not an intellectual exercise. Rather, dharma transmission is the ultimate mind-to-mind transmission from the teacher to the student of the Buddha's essence.

With the Japanese Zen tradition, the student is recognized as a successor of their teacher in an unbroken line of roshis tracing back to the Buddha. The student then becomes a lineage holder, usually announced publicly in a special ceremony, witnessed by the entire sangha.

Maurine's dharma transmission was unique. She was a student of Nakagawa Soen Roshi, who was the teacher of Eido Roshi, one of the Japanese Buddhist teachers who introduced Zen to America in the 1950s and '60s in New York City. Soen Roshi conferred dharma transmission to Maurine in 1982 during a secret ceremony with only the two of them present. I'm not sure why he did this; however, he was known as a nonconformist. In the United States, he taught women, something he never would have tried in Japan because it would break with tradition.

This peculiar situation is described in the introduction of *Subtle Sound, The Zen Teachings of Maurine Stuart [edited by Roshi Roko Sherry Chayat]*:

> *In 1982 Maurine returned to Dai Bosatsu Zendo (in New York) where, in a private encounter, Nakagawa Soen Roshi transmitted his Dharma to her. "Tell your students to call you Roshi," he said, and that was that: no ceremony, no authentication, no formal recognition, no lineage papers. He, in fact, said not a word about it to anyone else. It was perhaps his greatest koan for her: a transmission definitely "outside the scriptures," in keeping with his unconventional spirit.*

Soen Roshi died soon after, leaving her with no authorized confirmation. This created a rift in the American Zen community because many people didn't believe her. As a roshi, Maurine felt she was empowered to fulfill the duties of the rank, albeit without official recognition. Nevertheless, she traveled the country teaching and holding sesshins. She developed her own following, especially as a role model for women. Nonetheless, Maurine was anchored to the Cambridge Buddhist Association where I studied with her for many years.

In some form or another, I attended over fifty sesshins with Maurine. One dokusan experience in February of 1985, when I was thirty-three, was markedly exceptional and memorable:

I enter the dokusan room as usual. I prostrate myself, take three bows and then get up on the cushion as fast as I can.

I meet Maurine's gaze, without hesitation.

This day there is a distinctive look in her eyes.

She is looking at me . . . but not at me at all, rather into the depths of my being.

I join her. It is a link, a channel . . . perhaps it is a vortex.

It is like we travel through a condensed tunnel in a split second . . .

Then we are one. We merge.

Yet, beyond one . . . expanding outward as part of the infinite Universe.

I feel the energy of Creation coming from her—actually through her.

She is a conduit. We continue expanding until we are boundless . . .

I have never felt a connection like this . . .

Limitless . . .

The energy of the Universe . . .

The Power of the One.
We are someplace where time does not exist.
Then it slowly fades ... until we are back.
Maurine speaks. "I have given you dharma transmission as I have received it from my teacher."

The session was over. I was dazed. I returned to my cushion downstairs with the others. I felt honored—or something beyond honored. A new me, but not. Somehow, I was different. I felt free. And powerful—a Power within. As the *Tao Te Ching* says, "The valley spirit never dies, it conquers all." I knew from my Taoist studies this meant the Power within will always defeat the Power over. This is what I had been working toward and searching for since I was eighteen.

My Zen practice continued. It's strange—everything changed, and yet nothing changed. I expected my dharma transmission to be announced to the community at the end of the sesshin or to have some kind of confirmation ceremony with the sangha. Yet neither happened.

I returned to the routine of the Zendo. Maurine gave me permission to teach a Zen group on my own in Framingham, Massachusetts. Also, Maurine asked me to lead some of the sittings in the Zendo when she was away. I was bewildered—still no announcement, no ceremony. I felt myself doubting what happened. Did the dharma transmission actually occur? I knew it did. Nonetheless I continued to sit with the sangha at the Zendo.

My connection to the One through Maurine happened in early winter. As the end of the year approached, Maurine surprised me. She told me it was time to become a Buddhist priest. This came out of the blue. Why me? From what I knew, this was the first time she had offered ordination to anybody. I had not heard any talk about this in the sangha. She wanted to perform the ceremony at the end of Rohatsu—the intensive sesshin that ends on December 8, Buddha's enlightenment day. It was not the time for me because my father had died two weeks before Rohatsu, and my daughter was born four days later.

Maurine was persistent. In early 1986 she asked me again to be ordained as a priest. I remember the encounter distinctly. Outside of sesshin, Maurine invited me to meet with her in the dokusan room:

I enter the room. Maurine is welcoming, as always. We both sit on our cushions.

She speaks: "I'd like to revisit the question of you becoming a priest."

Even before Maurine finishes her sentence, I enter non-ordinary reality. I have a sharp vision.

I see a line of Jewish ancestors.

They are not my father or mother or my grandparents. They are dressed in the clothing style of the thirties and forties, mostly men in suits with fedora hats. The line is lengthy, extending into the distance directly in front of me, bending diagonally off to the right. There are hundreds, perhaps thousands of people.

I know none of them.

Yet, I have a knowing—these were victims of the Holocaust.

They all speak at once. Not with words, but directly into my mind, like a loud echo in a cavern.

"You are a Jew," they say. "You are not a Buddhist. Stay in your tradition."

It is terrifying, as if the voice of the One has come down from above and spoken directly to me.

> *In that moment I remember the words of the Dalai Lama: "People may study Buddhism but should stay with their religion of birth."*
>
> *The vision ends.*
>
> *Immediately, I share my prescient vision with her.*
>
> *"Maurine, I cannot do this. I do not want to restrict myself to Zen. I am interested in other ways of connecting to the One. I am a mystic. Experiencing the One is what I want to do. I love you. I love Zen. And I will never stop my Zen practice."*
>
> *Maurine nods and says nothing.*
>
> *I see she is sad. But in some way, I think she sensed I would refuse her offer.*
>
> *I feel something has changed between us. Something deep and profound is severed and perhaps broken.*
>
> *I leave in silence. I return home.*

Why me? I can only assume she approved of my abilities, my dedication, and my gift to connect with her and the One. Yes, I wanted dharma transmission. But I wasn't interested in the sutras or anything related to religiosity and the dogma of Zen Buddhism. I never wanted to be tracked as a priest. The responsibilities of a roshi didn't interest me. I certainly did not want to be seen as guru. I wasn't driven toward any of it. I wanted only to attain the skillset of a Zen Master. Perhaps Maurine misinterpreted my dedication and focus. I felt like I owed her something but could not give it to her. I was very sad.

As time went on Maurine began to act more formally in the Zendo, both toward me and with others. When I'd first arrived, the structure was quite informal. I wore a t-shirt and pants when sitting. There was limited ceremony. After Maurine's dharma transmission and recognition as roshi, the construct of the Zendo became more traditionally Buddhist, with formal religious rituals involving bells, incense, and robes. Maurine would host other famous roshi at the Zendo and would travel throughout the United States teaching.

We began to drift apart. I didn't frequent the Zendo as much because I had my own weekly sitting/teaching group. I continued intensive sitting at home. I had just started a doctoral program in psychology. I had my young children to help care for. Also, I had a healing practice of oriental medicine and psychotherapy to run. Gradually, our connection faded.

The last time I saw Maurine was at my office in 1987. She came to me for a consultation because she was having severe pain in her head. I could sense something was seriously wrong—she was ill. I told her she needed to see a physician to get a clearer diagnosis through imaging, such as an MRI or CAT scan. She listened to me. I think she agreed with what I said. Then she left my office. To me, we were still on good terms. I emailed her a few times to touch base. She didn't respond. Sadly, we never spoke again.

One day in the early 1990s, Maurine's head student, Deidre, called me. She told me Maurine had been diagnosed with liver cancer and had died. I was shocked. I hadn't sensed Maurine had cancer when I'd last seen her. And I was shaken—why hadn't she called me to let me know what was going on? It was like I had just faded away. Had I become invisible? Was Maurine angry with me?

Deidre's next question jarred me back to the moment. "Are you still practicing Buddhism?"

I responded, "Of course. I practice every day. I love the practice, but I am not an '-ist.' I love Zen, I am Zen, but I am also more. I want to explore other Ways as they come to me."

She continued: "Why don't you come visit me and my Zen group soon?"

Her group met in the town of Harvard, about an hour's drive away. Unfortunately, I never made it.

After I hung up the phone, I wondered, *What happened? How did Maurine and I drift so far apart? Why did she not tell me about the severity of her illness?*

I suppose a lot was going on at the time. I got busy with life and family and Maurine had the Zendo to care for and she was sick.

I had a flashback to that special day in the dokusan room:

I meet Maurine's gaze, without hesitation.

We merge.

I feel the energy of Creation coming from her—actually through her.

The energy of the Universe...

The Power of the One.

Maurine speaks. "I have given you dharma transmission as I have received it from my teacher."

The experience was real. We were both there.

So why did Maurine never publicly announce my dharma transmission? Because of that, I never mentioned it to anyone. I left the Zendo confused. I've remained confused ever since. What did Maurine mean by "dharma transmission"? Sometimes I question if it really happened. Yet, I remember distinctly she had used those words: "I have given you dharma transmission as I have received it from my teacher." The mind-to-mind transmission between us was powerful and life-changing.

Forty years passed.

I walked by a bookcase in my house. There was an energetic tug. I looked up and saw a specific book among many, as if it were calling to me. I reached up and took it off the shelf. It was covered with dust. The book was *Subtle Sound*. Then the memories started flowing.

> *I am back at the Zendo.*
>
> *Maurine is sitting across from me in the dokusan room, as we had done so many times before in Cambridge. We are both on our cushions.*
>
> *Intense golden light surrounds us.*
>
> *I was so overcome, I had to sit down on a chair next to the bookcase.*
>
> *I feel Power surging between us and around us.*
>
> *I am held in this light . . . so beautiful.*

I'm not sure how long this lasted, perhaps ten minutes.

When I could focus, I opened the book and read the introduction. It contained a detailed biography of Maurine. I was shocked to learn that Deidre and Roshi Roko Sherry Chayat (the editor of the book) were ordained by Maurine on the same day, December 8, 1985. If I had accepted Maurine's invitation to become a priest, I would have been part of that ceremony. *What?* I wondered. *After forty years, I now learn this? What else was hidden from me?*

I then read a few sentences in the book that further complicated my understanding of my dharma transmission: "Maurine left no dharma heir. Her transmission was not by way of an established lineage, not to select one or two. Her legacy was all inclusive."

This made no sense to me. If Maurine felt she did not have the authority to transmit the dharma and call herself a roshi, then why did she do both? There were people at the Zendo who wanted to make the priesthood their life. They were counting on her as a recognized teacher to transmit the dharma to them. That was the point—why else be there?

I wondered if this had happened to anyone else. It turns out it did. One of my master students told me about a man who studied with Maurine around the same time I was at the Zendo. My student passed along his contact information, and I called him to learn more. He recounted to me an experience similar to mine in the dokusan room. Maurine told him he had been given dharma transmission. Like with me, it was never announced. Even more confusing, he was told at the time—by Maurine herself—she did not have the authority to do so. He later chose to study with another teacher after Maurine died and subsequently received transmission from that person. I thought, *This is such a mess.*

The downstream effects of the unorthodox (albeit noble) practices of Maurine's teacher—Soen Roshi—are far reaching. Since Maurine's transmission was not a normal one, it could not be recorded or included in the lineage book as is the custom of established Zen tradition. This applies to my transmission, too. Also, after Maurine died, the Cambridge Buddhist Association, who hired her and owned the Zendo, would not recognize any of the people Maurine ordained as priests.

Did all this matter to me? Of course. How could it not? Her actions negated everything I did. For decades after leaving the

Zendo, I felt invisible and not recognized. I was ignored by my master teacher and unrecognized by the community.

For the next few weeks, I sat with all this. I thought a lot about it, too.

Nonetheless, when I was in the Realms meditating, Maurine was with me. When she appeared, she exuded loving compassion—as she did when alive—like no other. It is love from the One. We had a remarkable final shared experience together:

> *As before, we are on the cushions, in the dokusan room, in the Zendo, in Cambridge.*
>
> *We merge.*
>
> *This time I feel more empowered to ask her, "What did you mean by dharma transmission?"*
>
> *She replies, "When we sit like this together, I am transmitting the dharma to you. We are sharing the dharma together. This was how Soen Roshi gave me dharma transmission. This is how I am comfortable giving you my dharma transmission. I did not feel I had the authority to give you formal transmission."*
>
> *Suddenly, I have an intense, overwhelming experience of Grace, emanating from the One and encompassing both of us.*
>
> *In this moment, I feel seen. And validated. And so loved. I feel she is offering the answer to the koan of our connection and time together.*
>
> *Then, all my long-standing angst just melts away.*
>
> *I acknowledge, "I am sorry I could not give you what you wanted. I could not become a priest."*
>
> *She replies, "You must follow your own path. It is time to let go of all doubt and tell your story. Tell your students to call you 'Roshi.'"*
>
> *Then she fades away.*

All the love, dedication, discipline, and practice washed over me. Maurine's impact still echoes within me: all the love... all the love... all the love. It is with me after all this time.

To this day, I can invoke the essence of light, love, and compassion that emanated from Maurine. But for now, she is gone.

I am a mystic. Maurine was the first one to show me how to directly connect to the One. I later learned I needed to be radically free. I needed to follow any path that would get me there.

I am extremely grateful for my Zen journey with Maurine Stuart Roshi.

I will tell my story.

QUESTIONS FOR SELF-REFLECTION

- What have you concealed for a long time?

- What is repressed, hidden, or denied? . . . perhaps a belief about yourself, a memory of an incident, an event, of words exchanged, an injury, or even a death?

- What do you fear?

- Ask yourself: why am I afraid?

- What would happen if you told others about it?

- Where is the Power in holding back?

- Where is the Power if you reveal your story?

KOAN 2

I am having this recurring dream.

There is this lady, maybe in her forties, sitting in a chair. All around her are pictures and statues of what looks like Mother Mary. The lady keeps beckoning to me like she wants me to join her somewhere.

I wake up. Usually, I do not remember my dreams.

Calling the Souls

My business partner and colleague Darin, a psychologist and acupuncturist, came into my office. We were close friends and mentors to each other. We often talked about how acupuncture and psychology intersect, about how mystical traditions could fit into the framework of contemporary psychology.

This time, he told me about a shaman, a woman named Natasha, he had met through one of his patients. The patient introduced Darin to a psychiatrist in Rhode Island, who turned out to be a student of the shaman. He felt I needed to meet her. This was the strange sequence of events that led up to my meeting. To this day, and even back then, this was all too vague for me because there were too many strange coincidences for me to follow. In hindsight, I am never quite clear on how this all worked out because there was a cascade of events that led up to a fateful meeting.

Darin would not let up. He kept badgering me. He wanted me to meet this healer.

"Why?" I kept asking him. "I am into my Zen and Taoist practices. How would shamanism add to my practice?"

After a while, I got tired of listening to him, so I agreed to go to Providence where this shaman was seeing some clients.

We entered the backroom of a New Age bookstore, near Brown University. Darin is six-foot-eight. I couldn't see anything beyond him because he towered over me and blocked my view. As he moved to the side, I saw a woman. She turned to look at me. I was speechless. Stunned. *I realized it was the lady from my recurring dream!*

I felt disoriented and off center. I was shaken by an internal earthquake. Like a bolt of lightning, my world shifted—just as in dokusan with my Zen teacher, Maurine. It never shifted back.

It was *the* moment. Natasha looked at me, smiled and said, "Oh, my. You are the real thing. I don't get to meet many people like you. Look at the *violence*. All that *violence*."

I had no idea what she was talking about. I sat down in a chair across from her.

She continued. "You are a warrior shaman. You are one of those who protects the village from attack and will strike other villages to gain power. Your gifts are rare."

I was awestruck.

"You will work with possessions, dark entities who enter people's souls and steal their energy."

Over time, I understood why I was called to her. She told me I would work with darkness while she worked with light. Many times, she told me I had done this in prior lifetimes. However, in this life I was to be a healer of both light and darkness.

Natasha was a white woman from Spain. She said her father fled Franco and ended up in Kenya because he had a gem business based there. At age three she was adopted by the village shaman and was trained by him. I never knew if any of her history was accurate. Her birthday would change every year. Sometimes she said it was in May. Other times she told me it was in July. She said she went to school in Switzerland. When was that? I never got a date. Natasha had lived in Chile, Puerto Rico, Monaco, and now upstate New York. But that list might change the next time I talked with her. She was into shamanism and Mother Mary. Somehow, they merged together for her. I gave up looking for an explanation. I knew this: she was the real thing. She had lots of Power. I could feel it around her.

Natasha's work was all about "Calling the Souls," as she referred to it. To me, it seemed eclectic, shaped by Catholicism and, I assume, some traditions from Kenya. She crafted candles, adding Power and energy to them, the different colors signifying their unique power and distinct healing energies. Then, she talked to ancestors—souls who had passed—who gave her the information she needed. The main soul she channeled was the village shaman who trained her; he'd died years ago. Then she used prayers as incantations. Once the souls gave her instructions, she set up a healing ceremony using the candles for the patient, who often was not in the room. This is how Natasha "cleaned souls."

In the beginning of my training we would do the cleanings together. It was a triangle: each of us in our own homes on our telephones—Natasha in upstate New York, me in Boston, the patient at their home, anywhere in the world. Natasha would direct the patient to wrap themselves in a white sheet for the first session so that the negative energy in their aura would be transferred to the fabric. Then, the patient was instructed to get rid of the sheet right away, usually by burning. From that point on, without the patient present, either Natasha or I would light the candles she made for the ceremony while holding the healing intentions and directing the souls to clean the aura. There were a lot of candles. We would light twenty-seven candles each day for twenty-seven ensuing days, totaling 729 candles. This formula was for just one patient. Sometimes we worked on up to three patients at a time—eighty-one candles in one night, totalling 2,187 candles at the end of the almost month-long healing session.

I joined with Natasha via mind-to-mind transmission, similar to how I had connected with my Zen teacher, Maurine, in dokusan. We merged our minds and focused on changing and repairing the energy of the aura so the client could heal. We only used loving energy channeled from Mother Mary.

Within six months, I was able to complete this process for clients using Natasha's candles without her assistance because I had practiced the healing method with her many times over. In hindsight, I think Natasha believed the repetition would help me balance out my warrior energy by connecting with the compassionate healing energy of Mother Mary.

Natasha used other healing rituals and invocations, too. Most of them I do not remember because they never quite resonated for me. They seemed overly complex. I wanted the quiet and stillness of my Zen training. While connecting with Natasha's clients, I naturally could just *be* and allow for the energy to move as it needed to. I knew how to tweak it, like a conductor directing and finetuning the performance of instruments in an orchestra.

Natasha was psychic, gave healing readings, and cleaned auras by calling on the souls for guidance. As she said, this method really wasn't my style, yet somehow I believe she knew her training and the practices would give me the foundation I needed for my future shamanic workings.

Eventually, I used the focus and clarity I learned in Zen and applied it to the different problems Natasha would give me—just like I did with the koans Maurine gave me. In either case, I was given a problem and had to rise to the occasion by using my mind and energetic resources to solve it. Natasha and Maurine helped me discipline the uncontrolled warrior inside of me. My teachers helped me find my Power by offering me their structures. I used what I learned from them as a template. I felt free to shape them as needed, for my own personal growth and to work with my patients in my healing practice.

Natasha would give me assignments beyond cleaning auras. The first one was cleaning a castle in Switzerland where darkness had taken over. At one time, Natasha had told me she had gone to school in that country, so I'm not sure if any of this was related. I had never been to Switzerland. And I certainly had never cleaned darkness from a castle. She instructed me to do this remotely from my meditation room in Boston.

For remote readings, most psychics typically ask for a photo or picture of the subject. I wanted to begin the assignment by having a picture of the specific castle in hand. But I did not even know the name of the castle or where it was located in Switzerland. I complained about this to Natasha. She was a tough lady, certainly not a coddler, and never very sympathetic. I did not get a photo. Instead, Natasha held a picture of the place in her mind.

She asked, "Can you see it?"

"Yes," I replied confidently.

Knowing that I had many experiences with mind-to-mind transmission from working with Maurine, this wasn't much of a stretch for me.

So, for the next few weeks during my morning meditations, I worked on this. What was I supposed to do? All I knew from Natasha's methods was to Call the Souls. She would channel her shamanic teacher, and he would talk to ancestors who then gave her the information she needed. That was not how it unfolded for me.

Up until then, I worked with Oriental medicine and psychotherapy. I knew nothing about working with Power or souls. I had no idea there were souls that I could call upon to help me handle this sort of stuff. Unexpectedly, when I called the souls, they showed up. Some came to me as people, others as energies and visions. In the end, to clean this castle all I needed was to focus my energy on that fortress and wait. I then watched the souls do the work. It was all very strange, indeed.

For several years, Natasha and I continued to clean auras together, working with my patients. She didn't assign me any more buildings or spaces to clean, but I felt confident and capable of doing so without her. As time went on, most of the cases I worked with did not involve aura cleaning, although I did ask Natasha for her advice when needed. The cases I worked on got more serious. Darkness. Attachments. Possessions.

One of my clients, Josephine, came in for an acupuncture consult about some joint problems and other health issues. She was emotionally vulnerable, as she was just coming out of a divorce. She was a woman in her forties with a strong personality. I could tell immediately that she fit what I call an Aphrodite Jungian archetype—an innate energy that both needs and attracts men. It was magnetic.

To assess Josephine, I entered into the Realms:

> *I feel the predatory and parasitic energy of her current boyfriend, Dan, who happens to have a heart condition. He is charismatic and controlling. But there is more to it. I see his dark energy surrounding her, feeding intentionally on her. He is manipulative. I sense malevolence, too. I am somewhat surprised by this because Aphrodite-types typically don't get involved with or overwhelmed by this kind of partner.*
>
> *Dan is what I call a Destroyer, an archetype who uses dark power so as to dominate others. Also, he draws energy from others,*

like a sycophant. He is cold and arrogant. He is draining Josephine of her life force to sustain himself.

I told Natasha about this situation. She agreed to join me, as we often did, in the energetic Realms to make an assessment.

We coordinated a time to meet in the Realms: 3:00 a.m. I was in Boston. Natasha was in New York.

I entered the Realms:

I call upon Josephine's soul (although she is sleeping and will not be a conscious part of the working). I wait for Natasha to arrive. Then, I sense her presence. However, as soon as she arrives, she quickly leaves.

I was puzzled. I phoned Natasha the next day.

"Natasha," I said. "What happened? Why did you leave so quickly?"

I was surprised by her response: "This is not for me. It is too dark." I felt she was unnerved and afraid. She told me, "You are on your own; you need to figure this out for yourself."

This was a watershed moment: It was the first time I was called on to do this type of work without the guidance of my teacher. So, I continued working with Josephine, alone. Since I had no spiritual connection to my Jewish roots at the time, I really didn't have a tradition to inform me aside from my Buddhist training and Taoist leanings. These taught me to be in the moment and allow for the natural flow. So, I continued the work without Natasha.

I had been chosen by the Souls to take part in this work. I returned to the Realms:

I call on Josephine's soul.

Immediately, I can tell something was off. I have a gut-feeling, the kind when I encounter someone at first meeting where I feel inexplicably sapped of my energy.

Then I see Dan. He is feeding off of Josephine from what looks like a tube attached to her left side, in the same way a mosquito or tick sucks blood. He is exhausting her energy and fouling her reserves with dark energy.

I know I have to break the bond between them. My instinct tells me I need to create some space. By using light, I need to ensure that the whole tube is removed, like pulling up a dandelion, because if I left any part of the root intact, the invasive darkness would grow back. This part of the spontaneous plan seems right to me. Though I know there is more to it.

I have to trust the souls to coordinate and align what I need to do next. The souls are with me—in alliance with me—especially the ones that have the ability to see this through. I feel it. I know it.

I ask Josephine, through mind-to-mind transmission, to think only of love. If she visualizes golden light around her, it will give me a chance to move in between the two of them to break the connection.

I begin by raising the energy, like winding a spring to increase the torsion. As the energy intensifies and amplifies, a weighty pressure builds up. I know somehow this is the force needed to move Dan away. And then? It feels like a fast-paced rescue operation: A medivac helicopter swiftly lands and the medics rush to the injured person who is positioned and safeguarded by the capable hands of a triage team. My role is to set up the conditions so the specialists—the souls—can take action for the best outcome.

Next task: Open a portal to another realm. As I visualize this gateway, I move Dan away from Josephine, unplugging the tube. The Void acts as a vacuum, pulling Dan farther away from Josephine, closer and closer to the vortex. Abruptly, Dan is sucked in and quickly disappears.

He is gone.

I close and seal the portal. I have a knowing—it is done. It feels resolved to me.

The final undertaking is to repair Josephine's aura where Dan had attached to her. This I know how to do because of my training with Natasha. To me, rather than resembling mending a flesh wound, it feels like using mortar to patch a hole in a wall.

Admittedly, I did not know how all this worked. I did not know where the souls sent Dan, except that it was far, far away, beyond this world as we know it. At that time, and to this day, all I know is the souls are the custodians of the portals and the Realms.

I had to return to this scene and its momentum for several days until I could see and feel and know that Dan was definitively gone from this realm.

Later that week, Josephine called to tell me she felt much better. Also, she divulged some astounding information—Dan had suffered a heart attack and died in the hospital.

This was my first experience of shamanic Power on my own. I was merely the conduit for Spirit to engage. It was the first time I used my innate warrior energy to strategize and implement a healing outcome. Did I know what I was doing? Yes and no. I did not make a plan of action, yet I did set the stage for possibilities to unfold. I learned to trust my instincts in non-ordinary reality, which, for me, is to be in the moment and allow for the natural flow, just as I do in ordinary reality. That's what I now call applied Zen, perhaps with a mystical application. Most importantly, I learned then to trust the souls. They were the stewards and guides. I was in service to them.

My experience with Josephine foreshadowed the crossroad where Natasha and I would go our separate ways. I learned so much from her, especially about the effects of holding a healing intention and the importance of Calling the Souls as partners for working toward healing outcomes. I suppose I both absorbed and ignored her approach. Natasha would set an intention and then create a detailed ritual or ceremonial structure for dealing with a patient and follow it through. But she could be inconsistent. Often, she would completely upend her own instructions. I'm not sure if she was honing the ritual or just improvising and doing what felt right for the time and situation at hand. This seemed muddled to me. Her method did not hold the Power I would need to work with darkness, turbulent energies, and fierce entities.

In hindsight, I realize I created my own structure, modelled after that first working for Josephine. I sit. I look at the problem. I Call the Souls. I wait. I take action, if needed, with and for the souls. I believe my Buddhist training was a cornerstone to averting the notion of setting an intention for a desired outcome. To me, setting an intention is aligned with ego. I don't want to impose my desires for a particular outcome on the patient. Intention happens because of inspiration, not because of my ego. I only take action in the Realms if I'm called to do so. Otherwise, there is karmic residue. It's like when a fire doesn't burn clean, there is ash left over. That ash is a metaphor for karma that gets carried over into our subsequent lives.

As Natasha noted early on in our relationship, she viewed me as a protector, a healer of both light and darkness, with an aggressive temperament. Before I discovered shamanism, I was known for my fearless outlook with my interests in martial arts, war strategies, and physical contact through rough sports such as football and lacrosse. *Bring it on* was my attitude. I was like a moth to the flame. I wanted to face the fire and conquer any fear and tap into my resources with discipline. When I work in the Realms (both then and now), I get cold and clear, without emotion, so I can be totally in that moment to connect with the One. I act—or do nothing—as inspired by the souls. All of this is just natural for me. I didn't need to study or train to know how to be this way. I think Natasha intuited that these competences fit the profile of a warrior shaman.

Natasha showed me how to Call the Souls in the way shamans work in indigenous societies. It was a sequential process. The shaman consults with the ailing person, the patient. They craft a ceremony. Call the souls. Work in the Realms. Provide aftercare. Reassess. The crux of indigenous work is a shaman-mediated solo journey, whereby the patient relies on the spirit walker to intervene for them in the Realms. I expanded this model by working with patients through co-journeying, whereby I act as a facilitator and guide in a shared dreamscape in non-ordinary reality. The co-journey is my preferred method because I feel patients grow and heal when they are empowered by their own involvement in the process. Additionally, I have worked as a proxy for patients who are unconscious and unaware due to serious illness.

An example of this would be Travis. He was in a serious car accident. This can be a time when dark beings try to possess your soul, as you are weak and vulnerable. Travis's mother, Mary, was a patient of mine. She was worried because after the car accident, he entered a coma and had to be hospitalized. She contacted me to see if I could help. I entered the Realms:

I call on Travis. It feels like time travel. Kind of like the space trek of the Starship Enterprise.

I see Travis lying on a bed in his hospital room. I try to contact him. He does not respond.

I look around him to see if anything is amiss.

I see a dark being who has half-entered Travis's being. I cannot attack the being as is because that will leave half of it embedded in Travis.

Immediately, I change my strategy. I go into Travis's body. In effect, I temporarily occupy his body. I direct the souls to attack the being trying to fully enter him. I direct some of the souls to open a portal to another Realm where we can send the dark being. Then, I attack the being from inside of Travis as if I am him. This does not take long to do. The being flees.

As soon as I experience this, I leave Travis's body and become myself again.

The souls and I direct the being to another Realm, and I seal the portal so it will not return.

Other souls sit by Travis for a few minutes to make sure he is okay and will recover from his coma.

To me, potent shamanic workings can only happen by harnessing Power. Defining Power has always been somewhat elusive to me because from a shamanic perspective, it is ineffable. It is not something one reads about and then understands. It is something that is experienced, cultivated, and honed over time. It is complex. It is nuanced.

One my patients, Jake, was a curious guy. He often asked me how I work and wanted me to define some of the terms I use. After a co-journey, he asked me to define Power.

"Well," I told Jake, "It's important to first make the distinction of *Power over* versus *Power within*."

Jake asked, "Do you mean authority and control are Power over?"

"Those are components," I said. "*Power over* is driven by ego and fear. *Power within* is connected to the One and to the cooperative human spirit. It comes from inspired and often caring expressions."

Jake nodded.

I continued. "Ultimately, what we're talking about is energy. A helpful metaphor is to think about a house that is wired for electricity. This is our natural state: we are wired for Power. The electrical outlets throughout a building can be used to provide energy for—to power—anything that's plugged in, such as a lamp, fan, or kitchen appliance."

Jake asked, "What is my Power?"

"People can plug in to their natural sources of energy—using mind, body, and spirit—to power their talents, interests, and abilities," I answered. "Typically, most folks get stuck in fear, for lots of reasons. They block their natural connection to the One and they hamper the flow of their Power. Sometimes it can take many years to get clear enough to reclaim it."

My warrior spirit has been an important impetus in the way I harness and hone my Power for healing outcomes. I always had aggressive tendencies. I used the discipline and skills required for martial arts as a way to regulate those energies so I wouldn't hurt myself or others. Learning how to keep myself in check allowed me to use those energies as a protector and, in time, to direct that focus into shamanic healing. For me, Power is energy that gets condensed by my mind so I have more energy. The more energy I can concentrate into Power, the more Power I have. I suppose this is a Taoist construct, in the way the natural cycles of the earth loop to feed and replenish ecosystems whereby energy is continuously used and transformed.

I've learned that Power is not intention. Power is not ego. Power is something that, when amplified, will attract those souls who can align with me for healing work. This is why my daily meditation practice is crucial. I must cultivate a clear mind space that is free from emotion to challenge and resolve any influence of my ego. I must stay humble to use my Power—and all my warrior skills that are fed by it—for good.

I continued with Jake, "Ultimately, the Power is not yours. This is what I teach to all my patients. It flows through you. Ego attachments, in the Buddhist sense, bring about suffering for oneself and for others. So, to avoid any karmic residue, we must be mindful of the way our Power is engaged. It must be fueled by connecting to the One as the source and ongoing supplier of energy while allowing for a natural flow. Otherwise, it will bring about illness by draining our mental capacity and bodily resources."

Natasha and I worked together almost daily for about five years, until 1994, when she told me I was on my own.

I remember clearly when Natasha said, "Where you are headed is not for me."

Also, she imparted two insights which were prescient to my future approach to shamanic practice: "Strive for balance. Love is the key." Then, our contact became sporadic for around nine years. My last interaction with her was in 2003.

During the time I trained with Natasha, I made strides in understanding and using energy, although I really couldn't articulate it until much later. That energy had a signature to it, which I later identified as Power. Perhaps Natasha's absence was a divinely inspired nudge to tell me something was missing. I remember how before working with her, I felt out of balance. I had an understanding of darkness and many experiences with it. I did not see it as a polar opposite to goodness, but as complementary, like the ancient Chinese yin/yang concept of duality. I learned how to use the darkness to help people heal. Yet, in order to have balance, I needed a way to transform my internal darkness into light. I knew I could use such energy to help people heal, too. That quest led me to the discovery of one of the most potent healing techniques I use—transmutation—for transforming one energy into another..

I believe Natasha's attraction to Mother Mary had to do with the Christian focus on love. I think Mary was her anchor for healing through transcendent, loving energy. Also, Mary represented the transformative symbol of the divine feminine. Without doubt, my own strength—both internal and as expressed in my body—held the opposite energy, that of the solid masculine archetype. Considering Natasha's parting words for me to find balance and to remember how love is the key, I'm not surprised by the serendipity of my introduction to a healing model that became a cornerstone to my evolving shamanic approach.

One day, my friend Johan told me about a practice he had discovered called *Ho'oponopono*. He was an open-minded yoga teacher, always looking for ways of improving both himself and how he worked with clients. Johan suggested I attend an introductory talk on the subject on a Friday night in greater Boston. If I liked it, I could sign up for the weekend workshop. I was game. That night, I learned about how this Hawaiian form of shamanic work was used to help solve conflict arising in group situations, sort of like using a mediator.

A compound word, *Ho'oponopono* roughly translates to "bringing back to balance." In Hawaiian, *pono* means "balance." The origin story, or perhaps the mythos, tells about how the originator of the simplified system, Dr. Ihaleakala Hew Len, miraculously cured a ward of criminally insane patients by using this technique on himself to shift the negative energy of those affected. He worked on himself to heal others. I found this quite intriguing.

During the question-and-answer period that evening, I queried the instructor about the many prayers they were using to shift the energy for particular situations.

"Where do the prayers come from?" I asked.

He said, "They were made up by the founder of the system, Dr. Len, who had channeled them from a divine being for all of us to use." We were to memorize and apply them, as needed.

Also, I asked, "Are all the prayers based in love?"

When he confirmed they were, I asked myself, *Why would I need someone else's prayers when I could make up my own?* And with that, I decided I didn't need to attend the rest of the weekend seminar. I'd gotten enough information and the essence of the skills needed to continue working with this technique.

I was particularly drawn to how reconciliation—compassion, kindheartedness, and understanding—is directed toward oneself rather than to another. So, instead of sending love and light outward to someone, you work on the part of yourself that is hurting, wounded, or in crisis. In this way, the agency—the control—over the entire process shifts from focusing on an external circumstance or person, to working on oneself, internally.

I began sharing this practice with my own patients. One of them, Faith, asked for more clarification. "What are you talking about?" she asked. "It seems very confusing to me."

I answered, "For example, if you are angry with someone, the process instructs you to work with that part of *you* that is angry. As strange as it may seem, the other person or persons involved are irrelevant."

"Irrelevant?" she asked.

"If you can change your angry energy to a loving energy," I replied, "you then change the energy you project to the person you are in conflict with. It is like the reverberation of an echo. This shifts the entire energetic process around the issue and allows healing to happen."

I called this technique transmutation—transforming one energy into another. In mythological stories, alchemical transmutation refers to the conversion of a base element, like lead, into a precious metal, such as gold. Without doubt, psycho-spiritual transmutation yields a precious result, a higher state of consciousness and access to our true, unencumbered Self. The result is a person who is more free from emotional suffering.

Some years later in 2007, Joe Vitale in his book, *Zero Limits: The Secret Hawaiian System for Wealth, Health, Peace, and*

More, worked with Dr. Len to further simplify and market Ho'oponopono to the masses. They created a formula that was a redaction of the original process and the prayers to four assertions: I'm sorry. Please forgive me. I love you. Thank you.

I did not work with the traditional form of Ho'oponopono as designed and promoted by Dr. Vitale and Dr. Len. Like everything else I do, I adapted it for my own use, combining my knowledge and experience in the fields of Zen Buddhism, psychology, and shamanic practice.

I have come to realize my Zen leanings and my shamanic practice are deeply entwined. They are informed by my training in contemporary psychology. I was influenced by Charles Tart, an American psychologist and parapsychologist known for his psychological work on the nature of consciousness (particularly altered states of consciousness), and one of the founders of the field of transpersonal psychology. I was especially influenced by the book *Transpersonal Psychologies*, which he edited.

My Zen training instilled the important practice of mindfulness, of being fully present and aware of this moment. The Mahayana bodhisattva ideal embraces an altruistic paradigm to offer compassion to all, through loving kindness. With all of my shamanic workings, I always consider energy. I ask: *What is the energy of the present moment? What energies may be part of the situation at hand? And what energies may be absent?* This is one way I assess patients.

Ultimately, I want to steer those who have asked for my help to a place of empowerment by bringing to the forefront the energies at play. With a compassionate, mindful awareness of the energy dynamics at hand, I facilitate patients to find an inroad to their suffering so we can change the energetic focus, together.

I also utilize a well-known transpersonal approach used in psychotherapy and developed by Roberto Assagioli. This is the psychosynthesis idea of your mind being a boardroom where you identify all the subpersonalities that define you and visualize them as individuals sitting around a table. For example, around my table there is Father, Wounded Inner Child, Husband, and Healer, among others. You—the big Self—are the Chairman of the Board in this internal conference room, serving as the manager and director. Since none of the subpersonalities are real (because they are all creations of the mind), personae who are present are subject to control by the Chairman. Sometimes though, one of the subpersonalities gets out of hand and takes over the boardroom by ousting the Chairman.

My patient Frank questioned me on this way of thinking. "Why does it matter if one of the subpersonalities takes control? They are all me, right?"

I said to him, "This is not a healthy situation. For example, if the Wounded Inner Child takes control, the individual might cede to unruly emotional desires. Such a coup could create actual havoc in one's life. The Wounded Inner Child could direct one to say and do disruptive things."

"What is the remedy?" he asked.

"The answer is to put a halt to the upheaval by changing the energy being fed to the subpersonality who is serving as the rebel leader," I said. "Changing the energy of the subpersonality thus changes the energy of the Self and restores balance."

Frank noted, "So, loving the Wounded Inner Child will alter the dynamics of the power struggle because he is acknowledged, validated, and nurtured.

"Yes," I said. "In the end, the Self confronts and manages an aspect of itself in a gentle, loving way. The bottom line is that change is afoot because energy has shifted."

Indigenous shamanic models rely on the shaman to facilitate a shift. I do that, too. However, I facilitate my patients to fully participate in the unfolding of their mysterious mind constructs and self-created emotional prisons. By looking at the way we use our energy, we become more attuned to our inner mental and emotional workings and how we can free ourselves from any self-limiting patterns. By combining the psychosynthesis boardroom model with loving kindness and awareness of energy, I have seen the transformation of emotions such as anger or anguish into inner calm and tranquility. For many of my patients, this reconciliation has provided resolutions to long-standing emotional pain. When energy shifts, suffering abates.

The shift in energy is integral to the work I do for and with my patients because clearer and cleaner energy is an important and necessary path to claiming one's Power. Once I realized the combined—and profound—impact of identifying and shifting energy, I was able to work on myself. I transformed those rebellious parts of me that threw me emotionally off-kilter.

This understanding changed *everything* for me. Finally, I could address and heal the in-fighting that was happening between my inner selves. Also, it empowered me to enter into shamanic workings involving both darkness and light where I needed resolute confidence in my abilities, matched by an unfettered, clear mind. Transmutation—transforming one energy into another—is central to maintaining my Power.

I distinctly remember the time I came to this realization. My wife and I were in Colorado at a family-owned dude ranch, 8,000 feet above sea level. We were staying outside of Durango, next to a lake created by a dam. I was sitting on the porch of our cabin, overlooking the ponderosa pines and the distant mountain peaks. My leg started acting up just before we arrived, so I wasn't part of the posse who had ventured out that afternoon for a ride on the horses. It was a typical autumn day amid the southwestern mountains, with a clear blue sky spanning an endless horizon. The air was dry. It was quiet and peaceful. I was in a contemplative space.

Then, something clicked. I had an "aha" moment. I had a compelling discovery—*I can balance the energy inside of me, merely by loving those parts of myself I am battling with, resisting, holding on to, or just uncomfortable with.* I knew, without doubt, this was true. I was emotionally moved. Tears streamed down my cheeks. I felt such relief. And then I sat for some time with the wonder and grace of that extraordinary moment.

It is simple. Just love those parts. Simple is not the same as easy though, as it turned out to be much harder than I anticipated. In addition, this is not a one-stop cure-all. The process needs to be repeated until the energy transforms, which can take some time—days, weeks, months, or more. As I worked on this, I also needed to keep reminding myself about the energy I want to transmute because that vexing energy was something I created. I strengthened it with each recurrence. So, I needed to make an active decision to change it by feeding it something other than the sludge that supplies the mire.

The answer was love. I just needed to change my focus from any unhelpful and contrary muddle of thoughts and feelings to love. This is a kind, caring way to restore balance within oneself, because as with the Ho'oponopono model, the resolution is *only* about the conflict within.

To heal the Self, love the Self. It worked for me then. It works for me now. I teach it to all my patients. In terms of psychospiritual and emotional healing, the bottom line is this: When energy shifts, suffering abates. In hindsight, this technique—one where I combine mindfulness with compassion and the undercurrents of energy—encapsulates both love and balance, which is exactly what Natasha had instructed that I pay attention to.

As Natasha predicted, my patient caseload involved increasingly more difficult and serious circumstances to resolve. Attachments and possessions, dark entities who had entered people's souls and stolen their energy, became my niche specialty. That really was not my plan, yet it seemed it was my calling. Now with Ho'oponopono added to my healing toolbox, I had a potent method for supporting both myself and my patients. The focus on loving energy proved to be a tried-and-true way to get clear of emotional baggage and any negative, self-limiting personal narratives.

Ho'oponopono empowered by engaging my patients to contribute to their own healing rather than relying on me to do all the work for them. Loving energy added space to reveal the roots. It is like aerating soil: As you decrease the density of the soil and make it less compact, there is space for seeds to take root and thrive. I used to rely on pure Power when working with possessions. Now I could use the energetic opening that Ho'oponopono unlocked as an advantage when confronting dark entities. This was the case with my patient, Lore.

At our first meeting, Lore, who was a medical doctor, settled into the cozy couch in my office. During our short conversational exchange of pleasantries, I shifted my vision so I could see Lore and the Realms at the same time.

I see two sets of eyes looking back at me. One is brown. The other is black. Immediately, I know this is serious, and I suspect a full-on case of possession.

It is more problematic and life-threatening when an attachment has taken hold from the outside of another, which is what happened with Josephine and her boyfriend, who was emotionally feeding from her externally by an affixed tube. This entity was different. It was dangerously entrenched *inside* Lore.

"Wow, who else is in there with you?" I asked.

Lore laughed and said, "You are the first person in fifty-five years who has seen what is going on. I have been to many therapists over the years, and not one has gotten it right. They just tell me I am delusional."

Lore was referred to me by a physician colleague who knew her case was out of his scope of experience and suspected a shamanic approach might help. I was surprised by her lighthearted nature and impressed by her strength to overcome the persistent drain on her psyche over the decades. Despite the tireless, energetic interference from this entity, she created a successful life in terms of home, marriage, money, and career. Lore explained she had a long list of psychological issues and physical illnesses, culminating with cancer. Admittedly, I didn't listen fully to the litany of her troubles because I was assessing her energy and the Power I would need to extricate the unwelcome bond. The crux of this matter was the cause—the possession—rather than her struggles, which were symptomatic and would resolve once we ousted the intruder.

"Who's in there?" I questioned. "And why?"

It didn't take long before I figured out her mother was the culprit. Lore had been possessed at birth. Such a phenomenon is common with "helicopter parents," those who hover over children and control their every move rather than encouraging autonomy and healthy separation. In this case, it seemed her mother was a sycophant. Often, these predatory people possess their prey when they are in a weakened state, from illness or trauma. Some take advantage of the vulnerability of an infant. I believed that is what Lore's mother had done. Such energetic piranhas usually have their own share of physical and mental problems, so they seek a supplemental energetic supply from their offspring. Somehow, Lore had sufficient strength to withstand her mother's drain while crafting a successful life for herself. But it still took a toll, and she was tired.

Lore was eager to follow my instructions and start the separation. The first order of business was to disrupt her mother's feeding cycle by shifting any negative energy Lore was holding against her mother.

"Find the part of yourself that hates your mother," I told Lore. Then I instructed her to draw a picture of her mother on a piece of paper to capture her essence. "Now," I said, "direct all your anger and rage to the picture on the piece of paper. You need to release all of that anger first so we can then focus on love."

I directed Lore to burn the piece of paper as both a symbolic and energetic release. Also, this displaced the energetic bearing, rerouting a deeply furrowed pathway. Then I needed her to use Ho'oponopono to transmute any negative energy that she was sending to any subpersonalities of her boardroom that were angry. This weakened the negative energetic bond that was feeding her mother. Lore needed to send the love to that part of herself that was angry. The loving vibe then created an energetic opening, exposing the roots and allowing me to collaborate with the Souls to start the extraction.

As with any possession, I entered the Realms:

I call on the Souls. I open a portal and use a vacuum in the Void to draw the offender away. The Souls both power and empower me. They are the drivers, the proxies, and partners in this working.

Then, like a surfer in the Realms, I skim the vast energetic ocean, becoming one with the greater flow, feeling the waves until the right moment arises to ride the surge of a meaningful current. When I am surrounded and supported by the Souls, they are an army in waiting, preparing to charge in response to any ruckus.

I pause and then take action as needed until I let go of the swell and fall into that wave, as the portal closes and seals. The Power roils throughout the undertaking and then quickly ebbs and dissipates. This is when I know the task is done.

It took a few days of repeating this rite for Lore to finally be free of her mother. With de-possessions, most of my patients tell me they intuit a shift, like an emotional weight has been lifted, or they feel a notable increase in vitality. Often, the shift takes some time to permeate because a possession can become a comfortable connection. Once that's gone, some feel liberated. Some feel lost, empty, and alone. In any case, those who are released from possession need ample time to recover and realign.

For the soul who has been expelled, their source of food is now gone. Lore's mother was elderly and ill. After the separation, she weakened. Soon after, she was placed in a nursing home and died a year later of natural causes. I instructed Lore to inform me when her mother passed, so I could be watchful, should her mother attempt to re-attach herself after death. She did not. Lore could now continue to live her life, free of her mother's energetic drain.

Working with darkness and possessions were the main skills I developed over the time I trained with Natasha, although she did neither. She simply modeled how to Call the Souls and how she used a set structure for healing auras. Most importantly, I learned I had the ability to stand on my own when dealing with darkness. I shaped my own way of working that was very different than hers. I learned how to work in the Realms. I made connections with souls who were present for all of my workings. Also, I made connections with souls who would become present for specific workings and never be seen again. In each instance, I put my trust in a consistent method: I sit. I define the problem. I Call the Souls. I wait. I take action only when inspired and directed by them.

A few years into my training with Natasha, I started a doctoral program in psychology with a focus on inducing non-ordinary states of consciousness by using acupuncture, a healing modality I had then been working with for over ten years. As a baseline for my research, I used Stanislav Grof's holotropic breathwork model. Grof was a transpersonal psychiatrist who researched non-ordinary states of consciousness for exploring the human psyche, especially for healing and personal growth. My research supported the premise that acupuncture induces a deep, trance-like relaxation to lessen the sensory barrier between the conscious and unconscious mind. Over 250 group sessions with ten to fifteen participants showed that 98 percent achieved a non-ordinary state of consciousness in an hour and a half, compared to Grof's holotropic model which had a 50 percent success rate with three-hour sessions. Both models proved that entheogens are unnecessary for accessing a trance state. For me, acupuncture was also a gateway to the energetic body so healing could occur under the right conditions.

I was pleased with the outcome of my research findings. I was not surprised how clearing energy pathways in the body through acupuncture was one additional way to help people achieve a trance state. The natural extension to my thesis work was to offer my technique to the greater public, to those interested in doing their own personal healing work through shamanic journeys.

For the next decade, I partnered with a percussionist friend, Dana, who had extraordinary drumming skills. We hosted monthly gatherings for a dozen to thirty people at the acupuncture school, yoga studios, and other spaces we rented. The formula replicated my thesis work whereby we used acupuncture needles to induce a trance state. This time, however, I added captivating and mesmerizing live sound. For an hour or more, we led participants through a sound immersion, starting with Tibetan bells, bowls, and gongs. Then we amped up the energy with complex rhythmic African drumming patterns, followed by deafening silence, recovery time, discussion, and sharing.

My job was to create and hold space—not the space here and now but in another Realm. I made a bubble around the group with the Power that was generated by the drums and bells. As with any shamanic journey work, some folks experienced shifts in awareness or eye-opening, confirmatory information. Sometimes they just had a pleasurable experience and needed some time to process their thoughts and feelings while away from the group.

During one remarkable session, we discovered that time had stopped. I noticed the clock on the wall was not moving. I looked at Dana, the drummer, for confirmation, and he nodded and volleyed his gaze from the clock to me. Indeed, time stood still. There were no street sounds. Visually, the room we were in was sharply defined. Yet, the boundaries were fuzzy. It felt like we were in a time capsule. The moment seemed fixed and felt heavy for an undefined, extended stretch until it released from its suspension.

I told Natasha about this. She replied, "Well, what did you expect? If you take them to another realm, time is always different."

In the early 1990s the healing community was abuzz with the relatively new model of Core Shamanism, as researched and promoted by Michael Harner with the publication of his book in 1980, *The Way of the Shaman: A Guide to Power and Healing*. Harner had stripped away the cultural overlays of indigenous shamanic practices, using the drum as the technique for inducing the nonordinary state of consciousness. His course offerings and foundation launched a neo-shamanic movement for Americans to learn how to become practitioners. The New Age movement was in full swing, adding all kinds of occult and metaphysical techniques to the eclectic mix, including divinatory practices, love and light meditations, personal transformation, and other healing methods and systems.

Over the years, I have wavered in my acceptance of and connection to the neo-shamanic movement because I know full well that I'm a Jewish, white boy from suburban Boston who happens to have some advantageous skills that fall outside of the popular trends of Western esotericism. I don't see myself as a shaman, per se. To me, that is an earned, respected title steeped in traditions of indigenous communities. I'm a spiritwalker, a mover of energy, a facilitator of healing. I offer my life in service to others through my healing practice. I really don't like labeling myself. I suppose I am a shamanist of sorts, one who enters the Realms with a knowledge of shamanic practices to problem-solve by moving energy with the impact of helping people heal.

Early on, I realized my shamanic skills were unusual because I was not drawn to the approaches used by most practitioners. I was neither attracted to nor used ceremony or ritual. I have never used entheogens or psychedelics. I am not attracted to them. Likewise, they never called me to them. I am not attracted to indigenous modes of shamanic practice, yet I have great respect for how others have used their Power and skills for the benefit of their people now and throughout the ages.

Rather, I have integrated my learnings and experience as a doctor of Chinese medicine into the framework of shamanic healing. I believe disease (and dis-ease) is caused by an imbalance in the interdependent energy systems of the body, mind, and spirit. First and foremost, I assess energy. I Call the Souls for guidance; then I work in the Realms with those energies. Most people probably don't see me as an empath, because I present as a peaceful warrior who can be fierce when needed. Few have witnessed that aggressive side of me. Without doubt, I am highly sensitive to energy. I feel it. I see it. I sense it. I can be it and become it. I am able to transmute and use energy in service to myself and others.

In time, I no longer used acupuncture needles for inducing trance or even for working with my acupuncture patients because I was able to see and feel energy patterns. For example, one of my patients, Betty, called me. On the phone she said, "My doctor has recommended a drug I have never heard of. She wants me to take it. But I am afraid. Would you mind looking at this for me?"

Even though we were meeting remotely over the phone, I could see her, as if she were sitting on the couch in front of me. She held her hand outward, palm-up, as if she was presenting to me a medication bottle. Immediately, I slid into another Realm, assessing the vibration, scrutinizing to determine if the medicine was an energetic match for Betty. Then I made some tweaks to the drug's vibration so it would best serve her.

I could do this because of all the time I have spent cultivating Power. My clients would say I'm fixated on Power. I agree. From a shamanic perspective, illness and dis-ease can be traced back to the loss of Power. Indigenous shamans and the lore brought forward through contemporary shamanic practices attribute a host of situations that bring about disharmony. These affect the overall health of an individual: traumatic experiences that fragment the psyche; disrupted, important life connections; spiritual entanglements such as attachments, intrusions, and possessions; fractured lineage patterns and bloodlines; and disconnection from the natural world.

Over the years, I have dealt with all of these obstructions that keep people from being present and rob them of their own Power. Resolving this is often a complex undertaking because of the nature of psychology—conscious and unconscious motivations and wounds must be uncovered, unraveled, and comprehended. Often there is a twisted trail of hurt people hurting each other. There is no universal shamanic approach or remedy for this. Most healing requires addressing layers of psycho-spiritual discovery that can only be dealt with incrementally.

When I meet with clients, I ask myself, "Where's the Power?" The answer is usually ensnared in a muddle of messy human dynamics. The answer often harkens back to the ways we disconnect from our Selves and the One through ego attachments and the tangle of interpersonal situations. With this perspective, I saw a need for working with my clients toward self-empowerment. If they can identify their own energy patterns and the energy patterns of others, they can discover and cultivate their own Power in the world. As such, I formed process groups. I named them The Way of Power, a title I borrowed from the Tao Te Ching. It translates to "The Way of Power" or "The Way and its Power."

First formed in 2003, currently there are nine active groups. Some are more thematically shamanic-focused, while others lean toward psychological process. I set the tone, hold space, and teach about Power via reflection and experience. I endeavor to make myself vulnerable by opening up my heart chakra, extending my energy as a bridge to the One.

One of my patients, Jake, once asked me, "Where do you get your Power from?"

I replied, "The simple answer is, the One. The more nuanced answer is, through expressions of the One." I added, "My daily meditation practice for over fifty years has helped me hone my ability to calm and clear my mind of its chatter and connect cleanly with Source energy. Additionally, I transmute energy—that is, I neutralize any charged emotional energy—so I can use it to build Power. In the natural world, each plant or animal will have its own radiation of Source Power. Of course, the same is true for people."

Jake then asked, "Are you drawn to energies of the forest, bodies of water, and the mountains?"

I said, "Oh, yes, I can merge with them to enjoy their essence or tap into their energetic expression of the One. Then, I can use that to replenish my own energetic wellspring and increase my Power. I see animals as my teachers, especially the bear, wolf, and hawk. Bear is protective. Wolf fosters community. And hawk is a master of focus, a single-minded hunter."

I continued, "Brother Hawk taught me a completely new way of being in my Power. By merging with him in ordinary reality, he showed me how I could own my Power, too—both in ordinary and non-ordinary realities. He affirmed for me that it is okay when I get in an alpha-male, cold, dark, hyper-focused, clear space. Unlike him, I learned how to be loving at the same time, which has helped me find balance in my life and offer my healing services in a compassionate way."

I then related to Jake the stories about my encounters with Brother Hawk. One May my wife and I stopped for a couple of days in Manchester, Vermont. The leaves were about halfway out, making the trees lacy, and the weather was still crisp, the sun not too hot. In fact, earlier that week it had snowed a little. One morning, she noticed that there was a school nearby called the British School of Falconry. That was all I needed to know. She laughed, knowing how I'd react. We called and made an appointment for the same day. Given how eager I was, we were lucky that it was too early for there to be many tourists.

Falconry is a very old hunting sport. The Egyptians as well as the Babylonians and Mongolians hunted with trained birds of prey. It was also very popular in the European Middle Ages among the noble class. It was part of a knight's training to learn how to hunt with a bird. As I was to discover, this training for future warriors involved not only using the bird to hunt but also assimilating the way the bird hunted.

KOAN 2: CALLING THE SOULS

The trainer and I stood at the edge of a large field. She put a large, padded gauntlet on my left hand. The hawk had a tether on his leg that I held while he was resting on my arm. The first part of the training was learning how to cast the hawk into the wind and call him back. Around the field were perches about twenty feet high for the hawk to land on, horizontal bars where he would stay until he was called back.

The first time the hawk landed on my arm after I'd called him back was an amazing high. His approach and landing took my breath away. The bird had a three-foot wingspan and came in at a high speed. I thought he would knock me over. But the hawk weighed only two and a half pounds and was amazingly agile in the air. Brother Hawk stopped on a dime and landed lightly on my gauntlet.

Beyond this brief high, the most amazing and lasting thing for me was my ability to communicate with Brother Hawk. He and I became one from the beginning.

A few years later, we went to Scotland. At Perthshire in the Highlands was the main branch of the British School of Falconry. In Scotland, the laws are very different than the United States, and you are allowed to hunt with the hawk. Off I went. You have to understand, I am not personally into hunting. I have no objection to people hunting, but it is not for me. In this case though, I was hooked. It turns out we were hunting rabbits. Rabbits are a problem in the large sheep fields. They make lots of holes that connect their burrows. The sheep get caught in the holes and hurt themselves. Also, the hawks get to eat the rabbits, so I felt better about doing this.

In the Scottish Highlands, there are not many trees. It is all open land for sheep. When you hunt with the hawk, you carry the hawk on your arm. When they see or sense a rabbit, you have to throw them up into the wind so they can get the lift they need to climb high swiftly. The rabbits are smart. When they sense the hawk on the field, they signal each other to go and hide. But hawks are smart as well. If the rabbit freezes the hawk cannot see them. They sense movement. But the hawk knows it can scare them into running. As soon as that happens, it is a race to see who gets to the rabbit hole first. The rabbits escape most of the time.

The hawk would first scan the landscape looking for movement. When there was movement, he was drawn to it, his eye focusing on it. If the prey made the smallest rustle in the grass, he attacked. If the prey could freeze and stay immobile, he didn't see it. When there was no movement, he scanned elsewhere.

I'm the same way. I search for darkness and for patterns that are not what they should be. When I see dark forces or disruptions in a smooth pattern, I'm drawn to them. If there's a layer of possession covering someone's own energy pattern, if a person is trembling with fear, if someone's stuck in a dark cave unable to get to the lighted sea beyond, I focus on that. If no disharmony in the pattern exists, I move on. This felt like a clear connection between the hawk and me.

What struck me most, however, was that Brother Hawk's mind was totally clear, totally focused on one thing. Hunting, killing, and eating—nothing else. He was not like a dog or a horse, animals in whom you can sense emotions and thought processes. Here it was only one way. Notice, focus, attack. So totally clear. No thinking about it, no reflection on it, no feelings around it, just the Power itself. He was completely at home in his Power and completely one with it.

When I merge with Brother Hawk, I leave ordinary reality and enter the Realms:

I gather my Power. I start from a place that is cold, clear, seeing. I start by focusing out. The energy condenses, the beam narrows. When this happens, my body doesn't exist. I am just focused energy.

Where I differ from Brother Hawk is that he is just focused outward, with all the energy of his focus channeled narrowly on scanning and on his prey. In contrast, after I focus out, I then bring the focus and energy back inside so it expands. This expansion is from the heart. Now I'm in a place of compassion, loving and understanding myself. I gather up the loving heart energy.

When I'm there and totally focused, there's a sense of spacelessness, of infinity, of total connection to everything. Back in the Realms:

> *At this moment of Power and balance, seeing and compassion all disappear and I'm just there. Everything seems to expand—time, seeing, consciousness. I look at a plant on the windowsill and see vibrations around it and in it. Others may see colors in an aura, but I see the energy running through the plant. Then the plant disappears, and I see a ball of energy. I see the plant's connection to everything around it. Lines of energy come from the plant and connect to everything around it. It becomes more than a three-dimensional thing.*
>
> *When I'm in this expanded place, nothing is violent.*

What does this have to do with balance? What I learned from Brother Hawk was a completely new way of being in my Power. He was fine being in his place of Power, the cold, dark, clear hunter. He showed me how I could be okay in my place of Power, too, which for me meant go to that cold, dark, hyper-focused, clear space. But unlike him, I could also be loving at the same time.

I first thought being balanced meant to be like a scale, to reach a middle space where love and ferocity, seeing and feeling, being and doing were equal. Next, I thought that there was more movement involved, that I have different places of balance depending on where I am that day, depending on what the energy is like and what I am doing. Sometimes I moved toward the loving side, sometimes toward the warrior side, but keeping poised in either case.

All this is correct. Now, however, I now see another level. My place of Power may change with what I am doing, but the balance springs from my ability to love myself when I am in that place of Power.

Jake then asked me, "How does Brother Hawk's affect inform you?"

I replied, "Let me put it this way: Brother Hawk was 100 percent okay with being who he is. I realized Brother Hawk had no fear at all of being in his place of Power. He was totally focused and fine with being focused, hunting, and killing. There was no anger, hate, or anything else. He was balanced and ready to hunt and kill his prey." When I saw him fly out with total focus and clarity, I realized that I was not 100 percent okay with who I was when I was in my place of Power. It was too scary. I've talked of my fear of being hurt. What lay below that was the fear when the Power came, I was not controlling it. It just was. I couldn't plan in advance nor think ahead about what was going to happen. It just happened. But in the same way, I never knew what was going to happen when I sparred. If I try to get set for whatever's coming, I'm a target—I'm dead.

I had doubts. So far, the energy had been right for what a particular situation needed, but I couldn't be sure that was always true. It helped that the warrior code was ingrained in me, probably from previous lives. It would be inconceivable for me just to go and hit someone. Nor do I say, "He made me angry, so I'll just go after him." Still, there was no guarantee that I was doing the right thing, especially since the energy and the situations were always changing. The Power was just what it was at a given moment. There were no fixed structures, no rules, no planning; the energy didn't flow through me like a known substance. The energy was just what it was.

I needed to be like Brother Hawk. I needed to put myself in my place of Power and know it's okay for me to be there. It is where I belong. Otherwise, why would the Universe have taken me there? Yes, this is a little like an act of faith.

After meeting Brother Hawk, I began to do Ho'oponopono to myself when I was in the place of Power. This helped me clear any resistance or fear to being in that place. It also balanced me. It somehow opened my heart at that same time.

When I'm in the Realms, I allow the experience to just unfold:

> *I disappear into the Power; the Universe selects what balance point I need to be at. Sometimes I am just in that place of pure dark energy streaking out. Sometimes I am totally in my heart and holding someone in a loving way. And sometimes I am somewhere in between. I am wherever I am supposed to be at that time. Since I feel no resistance, since I totally accept what is happening, I do not build up any strange vibrations and so am able to stay in that place. The balance is the poise of being where I am at the moment.*

Jake asked, "Does the same hold true for people whose Power is that of light and love?"

I explained, "These are people who feel. Often what they feel first when they're with another is not the person's love, but their pain. This isn't a bad thing; it's the way these people connect to another person's heart. It is how they become compassionate. But it wasn't very comfortable for me, to say the least. Most people want to get away from feeling another's pain as quickly as possible. In contrast, this feeling of another's pain and thus connecting with them is where healers get the most inspiration. However, if they stay totally focused on the pain of others and only reach out and try to help others, healers and feelers can end up getting depleted and hurt themselves. What they need to do is love themselves when they are in this very powerful place of connecting—not back off, not wish they were anyone else, not fear whether they'll hurt the other person. That's how healers can stay balanced and do their work best."

"Do energy healers feel first and connect with pain?" Jake asked.

I replied, "Well, I see first and connect with the darkness. I would love to be in the light all the time, to love everything, but that is not the way it is for me. I need to be like Brother Hawk and be 100 percent okay with being in my Power."

In summary, Brother Hawk taught me an important way of working in the Realms. I don't decide the type of energy I will use. I am directed by the souls to use either light or darkness. When I see darkness, and disappear, and summon up the dark forces, I need to be able to accept myself, love myself, love the place I am in, and love the dark Power that flows from it. Only in this way is the energy balanced, and only in this way can it be used for healing and not destruction. The same is true when I'm working with light: I need to accept and love myself and love the light Power that flows through me.

As far back as I can remember, I was attracted to Power. As a kid, I couldn't describe it. But I knew what genuine Power felt like. Those with an honorable, powerful essence were often intelligent and street smart, not necessarily charismatic, and never set on manipulating others. They were leaders who had the best interests of others in mind and would always lend support with daily challenges of any scope. They helped others move forward with longer term goals. I was fortunate to have many role models in my upbringing; in particular, my father, many football and lacrosse coaches, and schoolteachers.

I lived near a large playground of about sixty acres in Newton Center, Massachusetts. There was an old church on site, donated to the city as a community center that we called the Hut. Kids of all ages, from kindergarten to high school, gathered to play ping pong, basketball, and outdoor games and just hang out. The older guys, counselors in their early twenties, would keep the younger guys in order. So, there was no bullying. There was no stealing someone's football and such nonsense. None of that happened.

All the cohorts, the younger and middle-school kids and then the adolescents, would move through their growth years with a connection to the Hut, progressing onward with their lives to college and creating their own families. The older boys served as role models for the younger. Most were kind, competent, protectors who helped, guided, and directed us. This rich communal experience at the Hut probably fueled my capacity to be compassionate, to honor the value of community, and to be of service to others.

In contrast, my experience with martial arts instructors during my teen years and early twenties was not as pleasant and welcoming, as those men were often harsh, self-aggrandizing, and power hungry. Nonetheless, I learned from them important and much-needed lessons in self-control and discipline, especially how to maintain restraint when under duress. I knew instinctively that Power over another was not for me. It neither interested me nor suited my temperament. As I matured, I carried with me a yearning to experience and understand Power, not as dominance but as command. I knew that beneath the thrilling techniques of delivering potent martial punches and kicks was a mysterious discerning which was responsible for the outstanding skills and control of the masters.

When I encountered my teacher Maurine, the Zen Master, I was riveted by her presence. She exuded a distinctive energy—a Power—filled with clarity of purpose, of full engagement and presence in the moment. Maurine set an example in everything she said and did. As the director of the Zendo, she was a respected leader and public figure. She had immense responsibilities for the management of the operation and would steadily lead all required activities, including the demanding eighteen-hour sesshins. Maurine never mentioned the word Power. She didn't need to. Her Power was rooted in and emanated from her commitment. She was focused on connecting to the One and fulfilling the Mahayana bodhisattva ideal of service to mankind. This was inspiring to me. So much so, that I, too, made the Zen precepts the cornerstone of my life.

When I met Natasha some years later, I did not see the connection of how my Zen training would serve as the foundation for my approach to shamanic workings. Natasha never told me outright why she called on me. I think she could feel and see the warrior energy that I embodied and the potential for directing it in the Realms in ways beyond my understandings. Most likely she sensed the clarity of my connection to the One I had cultivated through my time at the Zendo with Maurine.

In some ways, Natasha was a mystery to me. I never really felt like she was here in this Realm. Or when she was in this Realm, the particulars were ambiguous. Maybe the muddle I could perceive had something to do with her missions as a clairvoyant traveler, one who frequently traversed the Realms and would return to straddle many Realms at one time. Like a shadow creature, she was asleep all day and up all night. We would talk in the morning, before she went to bed. And I only saw her in person a few times as we would coordinate our shamanic workings via the telephone and then work separately, remotely. I never had any idea about the accuracy and veracity of her life story because the details were a shifting landscape. She was Spanish and supposedly lived in Kenya. Then she was in school in Switzerland and somehow lived in Monaco. Then she lived in Puerto Rico and had two sons who were born in Chile.

In other ways, there was clarity. Natasha held herself up to a strict moral code, probably one she crafted for herself from her eclectic travels rather than one derived from a specific spiritual tradition. She was committed to helping others heal, and as such, she was disciplined with the time and energies she devoted to shamanic workings. Her single-mindedness was the bond of our relationship connection. I never doubted her work in the Realms. She channeled her shaman teacher for guidance, who always seemed on target. She was a calm person, mostly quiet and unassuming, and then she would surprise me with some amazingly profound statements. We never had friction or disagreement. She was real. She seemed wise to me. She was powerful in her own way.

There was no intrigue about Maurine. She was the opposite of Natasha. When she came into the room, everyone knew it. She had a huge presence, but not loud or overbearing. She had a yang comportment that exuded she was in charge—there was no question about it. Also, she was a professional musician, trained in France, so instinctively she knew how to carry her voice and body in a charismatic way. She exuded clarity. Her energy emanated loving kindness. She radiated Power.

The contrast between my two teachers was remarkable as they had such different styles. The divergence was between clear structure versus the indistinct. Maurine was a predominant seer. Natasha was a predominant feeler. Maurine was decisive about most everything while Natasha partnered with her teacher for direction and then would carry out his advice. In terms of Power, there was a common thread—both were rooted in their firmly held commitment to purpose. I must have absorbed their perseverance and unwavering devotion to dedicating my life in service to helping others heal. Without doubt, they were both heart centered. Maurine was drawn to the Heart Sutra and Kuan Yin. Natasha had a deep faith rooted in Mother Mary. Both of the divinities they honored are figures of mercy and compassion who offer assistance to those in need.

Upon reflection, both of my teachers prepared me for this lifelong venture of cultivating Power. I have learned the world is all made up of energy. As obvious as that sounds, the nuance unfolds when one understands that Power is a potent form of energy. Power, as condensed energy, can be used or directed as one decides or is called to use it. There are many ways to build energy, such as Qigong, singing, dancing, and drumming, to name a few. But these tools do not necessarily build Power. Cultivating Power is layered, like the complexity of a tree, where deep and expansive roots are needed to nurture the growth of a solid trunk from which branches extend out and above to finer expressions. A robust, rugged tree is time-tested, taking years to mature and enduring the challenges of many seasons of growth.

As a warrior who has cultivated Power to use both here and in the Realms, I follow a code of honor, striving to bring my Power to the service of light, of healing. I comprehend the gravity and responsibility of using Power. It is useful because it can effect positive changes that lead to psycho-physical and spiritual healing. It can be dangerous because it could be used with malintent and to harm.

Maurine helped me anchor to the discipline and focus needed to clear my mind so I could connect to the One as the steady source of energy that is needed to cultivate and harness Power. Natasha introduced me to shamanic workings in the Realms by Calling the Souls. I honor them both. I honor their gift of service to me and to others. Their combined influence shored up the foundation for the contrasting and complementary yin and yang way I connect to my Power: dark, cold, concentrative, third-eye seeing and light, warm, encompassing, heart feeling.

I can use my Power to clear darkness. I can open an energetic field to the One that extends outward in an embracing way so my patients can feel safe to uncover their pain, suffering, and trauma. I can use laser-sharp and soft focus—at the same time—to assess the needs of my patients and encourage them to participate fully in their own healing and self-empowerment. I can open vortices to send away malevolent energies that drain and sicken people. I can merge with any of the elements of nature, including animals, to feel their energies and welcome their messages. I can soar with a hawk and join with her as she hunts. As a spiritwalker, I can call the souls and traverse the Realms. I am able to shift between this Realm of consensus reality to ethereal dreamscapes of non-ordinary reality.

I have honed my ability to use my Power for my own personal growth and in service to others. Without Power—a condensed energy I have cultivated throughout decades of practice—I could not do any of it. All of this may sound strange and inexplicable, but it is difficult to describe the ineffable. Yet, it is the truth. It is what I have done for over fifty years. It is how I answered an unplanned vocational call and how it unfolded.

One memorable day, my business partner and colleague Darin came into my office. Often, we'd chat in the free time between seeing patients. He was a trusted mentor and friend. Also, he was the catalyst and the intermediary for my first encounter with Natasha over thirty years ago. Darin seemed anxious to tell me something.

"What's up?" I asked carefully.

Darin then related to me a peculiar story from one of his remote patients. "So, my patient, located in California, just told me over the telephone about a vision she had about *you*."

"That's interesting," I said, "since I've never met her. Have you mentioned me to her before?"

"Nope. Not a word," replied Darin. "You belonged to the Iroquois nation in another lifetime. She thinks it was the Seneca tribe. You died from a bear attack."

"Hmmm," I said, both intrigued and surprised.

"Does that have any resonance or mean anything to you?" said Darin.

"Not off the top of my head, but I'll sit with it," I said.

Darin knew that bear was one of my spirit animals. As a transpersonal psychologist and acupuncturist himself, he was always keen to take note of spiritual themes and any evocative symbology. Darin thought I'd be upset by the reference to my death in the vision. I wasn't. I was interested but not concerned. However, after a few days of reflection, I still came up with nothing of note. Though nothing felt particularly off or wrong, nothing felt particularly right about the vision.

I knew something about the Iroquois from my history studies in college, mostly that they were a member of a former confederacy of First People in North America. They were located in New York, not too far from where I currently lived. I questioned if the proximity to my home could be of note. Immediately, I sensed no correlation. *Maybe violence or community are themes here?* I thought. The tribe was part of the Great League of Peace, which had some influence in the design of a representative democracy in the United States. I perceived no relationship to this.

The bear? I saw it as protective. And the symbology of death is often about transformation rather than demise. *Maybe this is about bear plus transformation?* Still, nothing. I concluded, all of this is interesting to me, but I didn't see the connections to the vision.

Since I got no clarification from probing my own psyche, I figured I'd ask Natasha what she thought about it. The next morning during our daily check-in, I told her Darin's story and about my inconclusive, vague perceptions.

I remember, clearly, Natasha's response. It was unexpected. It was profound. It was a wise decree: "Visions, visions. So, she gets visions. So what? Can she heal?"

In silence, I absorbed Natasha's statement. Her tone was telling, unearthing her practical nature. What purpose did the dreamscape revelation serve? In essence, she was asking about potency.

Her words stirred in me a deep knowing. I nodded my head and silently mouthed the question that has become my personal and professional refrain: "Where's the Power?"

QUESTIONS FOR SELF-REFLECTION

- What are your hobbies, avocations, talents, and natural skills?

- Where is the Power in your daily activities?

- Which of your pursuits deeply resonate for you?

- How would you go about these tasks in such a Way that they could bring you Power?

- How could you better serve yourself, others, your community, or the world?

KOAN 3

Sparring with a hand-and-a-half sword. Sometimes holding it with one hand, sometimes using two.

I want to move and flow with the energy, that is, the Power created when the two of us engage. It becomes an energetic dance. This is not about hitting or beating each other. We want to be in the flow of energy around us and to become one with it.

The movement of my steps helps create the energy and yields a hypnotic-like trance. I do this, over and over, back and forth.

I want to "own" him. I make my energy stronger than his so I can control this "dance."

Ultimately, I do control the dance.

I lead my partner into a position where he is trapped.

This is the important point for me as the teacher. I want him to be in that place of having nowhere to go so he will let go. I want him to turn and face his fear—that fear of losing, the fear of dying. That won't happen. But it will feel that way.

Only if he lets go. . . .

Then he will be transported to a different Realm, a different reality.

The sword is my guide. I use it as a gateway to the Realms.

This is a satori experience.

Sword of No Sword

I am often asked by my shamanic clients about my fascination with weapons. I can see how folks could find it difficult to connect what seems to be disparate modalities—a healing art with a martial skill. Through swordplay, I challenged myself to attain the same—or at least a similar—connection to the One as I developed from my Zen and shamanic practices. It was an amazing discovery, a gift, when I realized that by sparring I could cultivate Power and be transported to other Realms. In that process, my energy shifts in such a way that I meld with the energetic matrix.

To my opponents, I seem to disappear. To me, I sense that I am invisible. And, to my satisfaction, I achieve the same connection to the One I experience with my Zen and shamanic practices. For me, there is no difference between sitting on the cushion in deep meditation with my Zen practice and when I enter non-ordinary reality to call the souls for shamanic workings. It is all the same in that I am focusing my energy and purpose on connecting to the One. However, with my martial practice, I use a weapon to get to that place of peace.

The Sword of No Sword is a famous concept in Japanese swordplay. I first came upon the idea in a book written by Yagyu

Munenori, *The Life-Giving Sword: Secret Teachings from the House of the Shogun*. In the late 1500s, Munenori, who lived from 1571 to 1646, was the sword instructor and both a military and political adviser to two shoguns. He immersed himself in Zen teachings and practice throughout his life. His training formed the framework for a unique approach to sword fighting that integrated spirituality and encompassed human potential.

Munenori, acknowledged by many to be the greatest swordsman who ever lived, believed that one could control the opponent through spiritual readiness to engage in the fight rather than actually enlisting in combat. No Sword evokes nonexistence rather than a lack or deficiency of an armament for defense. The mind must be totally free and clear—of even the sword itself—to move into a place of mastery. As such, no sword is needed.

Munenori learned about the important principle of mushin from his Zen Master Takuan Soho, who lived from 1573 to 1645. Mushin is sometimes translated as "non-abiding mind" or "no mind," which means to be present while directing the mind to not focus on any one thing. That may sound like divided attention. Yet, the idea is to be aware of everything at the same time, never distracted or sidetracked by any one idea or thought. Mushin is the state of mind that is achieved when one enters the realm of the Sword of No Sword. This is why Zen was so popular among the samurai, elite warriors who were known for their unrivaled skill and stealth.

From a practical perspective, a warrior wielding his sword when cornered must confront enigmatic situations in combat to survive. On the cushion, as a meditative practice, the stakes are not as high. However, the result is the same—challenging the mind to go beyond its confines in search of freedom from limiting controls. In effect, that freedom induces illumination, a clarity of mind. For the swordsman, the koan is a crisis of life and death evoking a way out or through a dangerous predicament. For the Zen practitioner, the koan serves to free the mind of its influence. The koan is a tool to evoke a spiritual crisis through illumination as a training and preparation for satori experiences.

Like many of my interests, I did not have formal training in swordplay. I was self-taught. I did not have a sword teacher. I learned a few moves through my studies of Kung Fu and T'ai Chi as both of these methods have standardized moves, called sword forms. However, I did not get to practice sparring with actual weapons in a martial arts school. I took it upon myself to learn how to spar with a genuine sword in hand. My first swords were made of wood because at the time, steel blades were not made in America. I had both a dao, which is a single-edged Chinese saber with a broad slashing blade, and a T'ai Chi straight, double-edged sword. Definitively, I was taught Zen principles in the Zendo. Mushin was discussed, but never the martial aspects. Yet, I had a yearning to know more about the sword and explore its practical applications and beyond.

There is something mystical about the sword. When I place a sword in my hand, the weapon has a presence. It is not inert. It is not lifeless. Rather, I feel its vitality. When I spar, it emanates an active, vibrant essence, as if the weapon has a spirit or soul of its own. Sparring allows me to directly connect to this spirit.

The technique I use with my sword students is the same one I use with my shamanic clients: dokusan, the one-on-one shared experience between the teacher and the student. In this conversation, or lack thereof, we share the timeless moment to uncover what is most true—what is real—right here and right now. With my shamanic clients, the preamble may be a discussion before we access non-ordinary reality. With my sword students, we start with movements to raise the energy.

When I engage with a student, I open up a space and invite them to join me in the authentic moment as it unfolds. That moment may include shifting together to another realm so as to connect with the One. When sparring, we dance together in an altered state, without the intention of hitting each other or scoring points, as one would expect when sparring. We often transcend ordinary reality and soar together in a co-journey of discovery for insight or healing. Sometimes we just savor the beauty of the moment as we connect with and without our weapons. I remember vividly one beautiful September morning having such an experience:

It is Saturday, 9:00 a.m. It's t-shirt weather. We're just outside of Boston. Above us, thick, puffy, white clouds stand out against the blue sky. There's a light breeze. I am sparring with my students. We are working on letting go, on not using our minds to think about our moves. That is our practice; to let go so we can ride the flow. We let the energy we've refined carry us along—until one defining moment when I leave the group. Yet I am here and have physically gone nowhere.

I am soaring like a bird of prey. I am shapeshifting. My arms are extended, like wings. Unlike any animal, I am laden with gear: a five-foot, hand-and-a-half sword in my right hand, a steel gauntlet in my left. I am Brother Hawk. I am hungry and I am looking for food.

An energy shift catches my eye. I am drawn to a ripple inside the fabric of the Realm created by my partner's movement or the shift in his stance. I leave Brother Hawk, sinking backward through my torso into my legs. My trance state, once expansive and radiating outward, intensifies as it condenses inward. Now infused with this energy, I intentionally draw Power into me.

KOAN 3: SWORD OF NO SWORD

The light from the brilliant sun softens and swiftly goes dark. At first my arms are open, outstretched. Then my head gently bows down. My partner reacts by withdrawing, slightly stepping away. My arms draw inward toward the center of my torso, in a purposeful, prayer-like position, while the weight of the sword gives way to gravity as the steel points outward, away from me. I am on my knees, collapsing, melting to the ground.

It is all dark now. There is no space or place for light. Very dark. Deep, concentrated, black. Soundless and still. I sense the yin. I feel heavy and dense, as if I am fused with this profound darkness. I struggle to hold my body's weight. Have I become a black hole? Have I wholly merged with this expression of the One?

I can feel the condensed energy, the Power pulling my partner to me, even though he had just stepped back, away from me. He is caught in my vortex, like a net.

I dissolve into the consuming darkness. The sword and I are one. We have merged. From sword to no sword. From here to nowhere. For that moment, and for some undefined length of time, I am invisible.

It was not always this way. Thirty years ago, we would be outfitted with armor—leather chest pieces, fencing helmets, and thick, articulating pads and gloves to safeguard our forearms and hands. Most of the protective gear was borrowed from hockey and lacrosse because we wanted the material to be flexible, lightweight, and relatively inexpensive. We used swords made of metal; however, we mostly practiced with shinai kendo swords made of bamboo because they were more bendable and less likely to cause injury. At that time, I did not have the skill to bring folks along on a journey to non-ordinary reality, as that was an advanced concept beyond my understanding. My focus was exploring which martial arts resonated for me and learning their foundational concepts.

Since the first time I witnessed martial arts, I was instantly and eagerly drawn to know more about them. In suburban Boston during the middle 1960s, there were few places to learn martial arts. The choice was limited to either judo or karate. I thought judo looked a lot like wrestling, while karate had kicking and punching. At the age of fifteen, my aggressive, male adolescent body wanted to kick and punch, so I chose karate and found a dojo nearby our home. As I recall, there were no other kids or women in the class, just adult men. That was fine with me, since I was bigger than most of them and this presented an appealing challenge for me to overcome.

I liked the *kata* (forms in Japanese) because they helped me solidify my understanding of the method and build stamina. As much as I liked the forms, I was an unapologetic zealot with sparring. In this karate school, most beginners did not spar, as that was a proficiency given to only the upper-level students. Somehow, I ended up sparring from the beginning—with black belts. I don't think it was necessarily my skill level that got me in with the sparring cohort. Rather, I think it was because I liked body contact and was not afraid to get hit. I'm told that when I spar, I swiftly enter a trance state, my eyes glow with exhilaration, and I beam with an ear-to-ear smile. There's something about the challenge of combining mental strategy and physical skill that draws me in with abandon. I was the same way with football.

Growing up, I felt out of control. I was getting bigger and stronger, but I was not sure how to set physical limits and manage my temper. Contact sports became my outlet because they gave me ample occasion to hit people. The problem escalated when I wanted to hurt people, most likely as an expression of my unresolved and untethered anger. Fortunately, my parents instilled in me a keen sense of right and wrong, so I knew I had to get control of both my body and mind. Sports, and then martial arts, provided outlets for self-control.

One day, in the fall of 1971, at the age of nineteen when I was a sophomore in college, I was out for a walk near the Cambridge Rindge Technical High School. In the playground next to the school, I saw an Asian man carefully executing, what seemed to me at the time, strange martial movements. I was so transfixed by the slow movements that had seemingly no hard muscle recruitment. I just had to stop and watch him, as my mind reeled with questions about the mechanics of the technique. Another day, I noticed this slight man with glasses warming up by the stairwell to a basement on a building at the edge of the park. He was stretching his leg out, with his foot on the railing. He was making, what seemed to me, peculiar, high-pitched, sing-song, in-and-out breathing sounds that were almost comical.

When he took a break, I approached him. I knew T'ai Chi was practiced outside in the public parks in China. It is a tradition to ask the teacher if you can join in because it raises their rank when they have lots of people who want to work with them.

I asked, "Would you mind if I followed along?"

Chen (I later learned that was his name) warmly smiled. He said, "Sure."

I was ecstatic.

That was the day I discovered the internal martial art of T'ai Chi Chuan, a self-paced system of slow, smooth, and continuous movement supported by deep, focused breathing. We practiced each week, while I also continued my studies of Shaolin, a form of Kung Fu, in the afternoons. I learned that Chen lived across the street from the park, and he was new to this country, a graduate student at MIT studying engineering. He was a student of the famous Wang Yen-nien, one of the most accomplished teachers in Taiwan at the time. He was a man of few words. His English skills were passable, though I don't think he felt comfortable having full conversations at the time.

Chen had a unique way of teaching. Mostly, there was not much conversation between us. When it came to T'ai Chi, he offered little to no explanation. I simply followed his movements across the field, back and forth, over and over. Then, Chen would show me how to link the moves into a form. This was our practice—repetition, so as to deepen the form. These forms were created in the 1920s as a popular form of Chinese exercise to make the martial arts more accessible to the public. From my other experiences with sports, I knew that to improve, I had to take responsibility for my own performance by keenly discerning for myself what I needed to hone. As I learned more about T'ai Chi, I was attracted to the whole-body and whole-mind discipline and training that was needed to learn even the basics.

College was demanding, as expected, and my time was limited, so I had to choose between playing football or continuing with martial arts. I figured my enthusiasm and commitment to football would carry over from high school, where we won the Massachusetts State Division One title two years in a row. I tried out for the freshman team. In the 1970s freshmen were not eligible for varsity, which meant we were in training for a year before we could play against the other teams. The coach knew my father from his time at Harvard. My father was an All-American—an outstanding player with a stellar record. And my cousin, who was a senior, was on the team. The expectation was that I would further the family legacy.

I attended just two practice sessions with the team. I left unfulfilled. Whatever I was searching for was not there. Looking back, I didn't know I was a mystic, seeking a connection to the One. I didn't know what that word meant, and I would have had no idea how to go about making such a connection even if I did. I simply had a yearning for more. So, I decided to stop playing football and focus solely on marital arts.

I joined a club at school that taught southern Shaolin. Up to that point, I had been studying an Okinawan style. Both the southern Chinese and Okinawan styles were known as external or hard styles in that they required significant muscle exertion and sparring for punching and kicking. The Chinese style was more acrobatic. It felt awkward to me because it really was not suited to my body type.

I stayed in this club all four years of college, rising to the highest rank in my senior year when I became the head of the club. I was pleased with my accomplishment, yet there was still something elusive, something missing. As I progressed through the levels, the style became more gymnastic. The agility required seemed more like a barrier for my burly size and build, a hurdle I could not overcome. Also, I was hearing more buzz about internal martial arts being taught in the Boston area.

Chinese martial arts are generally divided into two styles: internal and external. These labels help describe distinctive approaches to training for honing practical fighting skills and generating Power. The external or "hard" martial arts focus on overall physical strength, which includes cardiovascular fitness with notably fast, explosive movements channeled through activated muscle to effectively pummel the opponent. Internal or "soft" martial arts use a relaxed control supported by relaxed leverage. Body alignment and mental/muscular tension are gauged to bring about efficient transference of Power so as to redirect the energy that is coming at you. The consideration of biomechanics and physics creates fluid movements to carry momentum from one move to the next to undermine opponents swiftly and efficiently. In actuality, no martial art is exclusively hard or soft, as both require the mastery and balance of both inner and outer principles to be effective.

Internal martial arts combined body and mind with a spiritual foundation. This intrigued me. It called to me. I often wondered if the draw to martial arts was rooted in something beyond me in the here and now. I think I was a warrior in many lifetimes. But at this point in my life, it was too early to know. That's when I discovered Taoism.

In actuality, I knew about Taoism from an academic perspective. My undergraduate major—ancient East Asian Chinese history—revealed my fascination with antiquity and my selective interests. When I encountered Chen practicing T'ai Chi in the park, I was walking home from one of my regular visits to the Harvard-Yenching Institute, a foundation dedicated to Asian studies.

I was drawn to Taoist philosophies outside of any liturgical frameworks, such as those that involved purification rituals and offering rites to deities. The concept of self-cultivation—the development of one's own mind and capacities—was already a driving force within me. I was no stranger to unwavering discipline and directed focus. When I wanted to know about something, I committed wholeheartedly. The yin and yang model of duality made sense to me, as did learning how to become one with nature by following the inherent flow as seen and experienced in the natural world.

I could say that I was a nature boy, of sorts, as a kid. I sat under trees to talk and commune with them (perhaps a foreshadowing of my shamanic interests and abilities). I would hike often with friends in the White Mountains of New Hampshire.

KOAN 3: SWORD OF NO SWORD

I enjoyed tent camping. I trained in survivalist techniques. I was drawn to streams, rivers, and the ocean, connecting in a profound way to the currents, waves, and tides. The link of Taoism and nature just made sense to me. As with nature, nothing in Taoist philosophy is fixed because everything has its own flow and is everchanging. As such, I effortlessly embraced both the physical and mental fluidity required to succeed with internal martial arts, those not specifically practiced to defeat and defend.

Without doubt, I was fascinated with martial arts. I enjoyed the physicality. I liked knowing that I could defend myself if need be. I was quite mesmerized by those artists who had achieved a high-level of performance and skill. I aspired to be my best. Throughout my college years, I enjoyed watching martial arts flicks as I worked on improving my own skill set.

On Fridays after classes got out, a group of my buddies and I would venture down to Chinatown in Boston to have dinner and watch a movie at the local theater that often showed martial arts flicks. Those films were typical of the genre: somewhat tacky and filled with hand-to-hand combat action, chase scenes, and stunt work. In Boston, most of the viewers were from South China and spoke only the Cantonese dialects. Our group was just a handful of the non-Asians there and the dialogue was always in Mandarin with both English and Chinese subtitles. Even though I couldn't understand the language spoken around me and on the screen (neither could the Chinese!), I found the visuals captivating, especially the flow and excitement of the fight choreography. Yet the true allure for me was knowing there was budding potential. I could learn how to cultivate the interior mindset needed to execute such moves.

Simplicity. Patience. Going with the flow. Letting go. Harmony. These were some of the important concepts I would frequently discuss with my soon-to-be Taoist mentor, Paul Gallagher. With him as a guide I learned about the bridge between martial arts and my future work in non-ordinary reality to help people heal (this was a decade before I met my shamanic teacher, Natasha). With its interplay between the yin and yang, I learned about Taoism as the indigenous shamanic tradition of China. Was this link fate, karma, or coincidence?

Some years later, Paul and I were in Chinatown, not far from the movie theater, because Paul, an herbalist, needed some specialty herbs. After we ran his errand, we walked across the nearby theater district to the public gardens. It was a warm spring day. All the flowers in the well-groomed and tended beds were in bloom, particularly the irises and tulips. They were magnificent. Tourists and locals walked the park, savoring the lovely weather. The iconic swan boats were gently gliding as people paddled across the picturesque pond. We found an empty bench along the path and sat.

I posed a question to Paul. As we often did, we engaged in a deep, meaningful, exploration. "Is there *one* teacher for each of us who could lead us to all the secrets of the Universe?"

Paul replied, "That's a tall order to consider."

I retorted, "Do you think we both hold idealistic, unattainable paradigms?!"

We both laughed out loud and then got quiet. We observed the manicured grass and trees, the lighthearted activity all around us flanked by the bustle of the city streets.

I then said, "You know, Paul, I think we always knew the answer, like two old Taoist souls pondering the origins of the word *Tao*, itself. Of course, Tao translates to 'Way.'"

Paul said wisely, "We each must find our own Way, our own path."

Yes, I thought, *we already knew the profound truth. We had a deep knowing.*

It was 1976. It was the Year of the Dragon per Chinese astrology. I was born in another Year of the Dragon, and 1976 was a pivotal year for me—the Chinese would say it was auspicious—because my career and life paths were unfolding through a deep dive into Taoist studies with Paul. I had discovered Chinese Medicine more than a year before. This type of energy healing was both a practical application and an extension of my fascination with Asian culture.

Our chat on the park bench foreshadowed the development of my own approach. That method, which is rooted in Taoist flow, I later called Radical Freedom. It was the basis of my sword teaching style and how I ultimately would work with all my shamanic patients. Shortly after meeting Paul, he would introduce me to my Zen teacher, Maurine. The mid-seventies were a cascade of undertakings and connections with people who had considerable influence on my life calling. Paul and Taoism. Acupuncture. Maurine and Zen. All of this transpired not by design, but through serendipity, abiding with the Taoist principle of going with the flow. My initial magnetic draw to martial arts and the allure of my college interests in Asian studies were like a forest upwelling feeding a widening stream and stronger downriver current.

I met Paul at the New England School of Acupuncture, where I was on staff in 1976. He was taking a class in Chinese Medical Theory. Later, both of us were enrolled in the Chinese Herbal

Medicine course. We connected instantly. It was like we had known each other for many lifetimes. Our connection was mind to mind, heart to heart, always pleasant and filled with joy. Each week, I was delighted to see him, and we would chat before and after class like old friends who had been apart for a long time, mostly about Taoist martial arts and cultivation. Paul was a bright, articulate, eager student who had studied the subject matter independently for many years. I think he was taking the classes to reaffirm the medical theories he already knew. Paul was a scholar who immersed himself in Asian studies. In contrast, I was more of a fighter with a passion to learn about the mechanics and spiritual aspects of the martial use of the body. I just knew we had a future path to share together.

He was a fascinating man. When we met, Paul was studying at Harvard for a doctorate in Russian literature. Yet, in my opinion, Paul was one of the foremost Taoist scholars in the country. He spoke and read both the ancient and modern Chinese languages. He intimately knew seemingly everything about the Chinese: their history, customs, cuisine, social etiquette, martial arts, and philosophy of medicine. He was not a dry academic. He was much more than an observer and critic. Rather, he lived his life by following a traditional Taoist path.

Traditional Taoist practice is informal, the written account dating back to late fifth century BCE, as is recognized in Lao Tzu's *Tao Te Ching* whereby a man ventures off to be alone in the woods or mountains to live in harmony with nature. This is similar to other ascetic philosophies: the Sufi Muslim fakir who places his trust in God to manifest everything he needs, including food, shelter, and community connections; Siddhartha Gautama, the fifth-century BCE Buddha who renounced his noble station for austerity and simplicity; Socrates the Ancient Greek philosopher who questioned everything; and the solitary Henry David Thoreau who communed with nature.

All of these mystics were seeking a deeper connection to the One by renouncing their ego needs and entrusting the rhythms of the life cycle as expressed through the unfolding flow of nature. Paul, like me, was not attracted to the more organized type of Taoism that involved liturgical foundations to support religiosity and a hierarchy of priesthood with scriptures, doctrines, rituals, commemorative statues, monasteries, and temples. These underpinnings were a reaction to the arrival of Buddhism in China.

When I met Paul, he was living in South Hadley, Massachusetts, located in the scenic Pioneer Valley. This part of western Massachusetts is situated along the eastern bank of the Connecticut River and the southern slope of the Mount Holyoke Range. The first time I ventured out to visit him, Paul suggested we have lunch. I assumed we'd be going out to a restaurant to dine. To my surprise, we went foraging for wild plants in the fields behind his house, which we then cooked and ate. The environment was ideal for studying Taoist texts and martial arts forms, which Paul would do in an addition he built onto his house. He called it the Wu Ming Academy. *Wu Ming* translates from Chinese to English to "no name," a perfect example of how Paul lived the Taoist philosophy, disavowing a hierarchical view of the Self and society.

Paul introduced me to Ray Hayward. Ray was eighteen when I met him. I am eight years older than Ray. Paul is eight years older than me. Eight in Taoism represents the eight cardinal directions. We used this coincidence as a distinguishing bond of our friendship. We became brothers, akin to a fraternity: younger, middle, and elder. In many ways, we were the proverbial three musketeers in that our alliance was bound by our commitment to striving to do our best while learning and honing our skills.

Both Paul and Ray were students of the famous T'ai Chi teacher T.T. Liang. Paul edited and translated Master Liang's book, *T'ai Chi Ch'uan: For Health and Self-Defense*. Ray was especially close to Master Liang, somewhat like his adopted son who then became his first certified disciple. Ray had mastered all of his teacher's teachings. This honor is similar to the Zen Buddhist concept of dharma transmission, where there is an acknowledgment of the deep ties between teacher and student including a comprehensive transmission of knowledge.

Once, Master Liang, who was more Buddhist than Taoist, told Paul that he shouldn't call his school the Wu Ming Academy because the translation from Mandarin to English of "No Name" then meant it just didn't exist. In essence, you couldn't teach something from nowhere. I viewed this as a bemusing riddle, akin to a koan, something I would encounter during my future Zen studies for unraveling boundless truths about myself and the world.

Ray and I shared many hours working with push hands, a training routine practiced by two people in internal Chinese martial arts used to hone stability and kinesthetic acuity through arm and footwork drills. Push hands is a stylized method to learn how to spar with internal martial arts. It is the foundation for freestyle fighting. Ray knew a lot about the various forms from his experience studying with many teachers throughout the years. He was my instructor and practice partner in learning the sword, long knife, double long knife, and spear. With his breadth of knowledge, he subsequently authored several books on martial arts.

Ray was our hub of community connections with the martial arts masters. He introduced me to Leung Kay-chi, a Chinese master of Shaolin Kung Fu and the internal styles of Bagua and Hsing-I. By coincidence (or perhaps cosmic design), Leung, a master teacher with a notable lineage who impressed us with his forms, knew T.T. Liang. Both lived in Taiwan. Leung's forms were deliberate, choreographed patterns of movements that we practiced again and again so as to master their fine details. As president of the acupuncture school, I arranged for Master Leung to come to Boston to teach some seminars a couple times each year, where he eventually gained permanent residency in the United States. Ray and I took all his classes and were fortunate to have private lessons, too. At that time, it was difficult to find a Bagua and Hsing-I teacher, so I was honored to study with a man with such an impressive background.

With Paul, I studied animal frolics (ancient Chinese exercises that help cultivate health and longevity) and a host of other topics, such as diets from the Taoist perspective, Chi Kung, meditation techniques, skills for transmuting Power, and ways of connecting with the One. It was Paul who brought me to the Cambridge Buddhist Association where I would meet my Zen teacher, Maurine Stuart. Our friendship was so special that I asked him to be the best man at my wedding.

Ray, Paul, and I were kindred spirits in our quest to comprehend, refine, and innovate our practice. Our synergy was unparalleled. This time of learning was a profound and important part of my life. It was seven wondrous years of intellectual, physical, and spiritual discovery. True to the Taoist philosophy of flow and cycles, our season together waned and came to an end in 1983. Paul moved to Vermont and then a few years later settled in Asheville, North Carolina. Ray, having earned the title of *Sifu*, an honorable designation given to skilled teachers, moved to Minneapolis, Minnesota, specifically to be with T.T. Liang and start his own martial arts school. My life focus shifted toward family when my first child was born. Also, I left the New England

School of Acupuncture to immerse myself in my healing practice full time.

Over time, I gravitated toward practicing mostly with weapons, particularly the sword and the spear. Every time I hold a sword in my hand—ever since the first time in 1970—something peculiar and transcendent happens to me. The metal feels alive in my hand such that the joining of flesh and steel becomes a mystical experience. At first, I felt energy coursing through me and into the sword. With practice, I found I needed to let the energy flow through me, to guide me and show me a new Way. This was a breakthrough, eye-opening epiphany that certainly was influenced by my Asian studies.

From Taoism I learned to go with the flow. From Zen philosophy I learned to be open to the satori experience, to allow limitless moments of insight and clarity. My Taoist and Zen studies led me to the possibility of many crossroads. Lao Tzu taught how the path of life is in constant motion and flux. All Buddhist teachers underscore the concept of impermanence, that everything is subject to change. Nothing lasts forever. I came to understand how my martial arts practice could be a journey that led to any path aligned with an intention for a deeper connection to the One. Why? Because, for me, complacency hindered growth and innovation. This perception, which really was an instinct, congealed into a method one of my advanced students coined as Radical Freedom.

KOAN 3: SWORD OF NO SWORD

The designation Radical Freedom at first glance may construe a sense of disorder or chaos, akin to anarchy. In actuality, the independence—the freedom—is a way of transcending known structures. The radical approach eliminates or surpasses any learned experience or known boundaries.

Martial arts are taught through repetition. Frequent skills practice trains the mind and body for a keen awareness of proven tactics that bring about the desired result, to guard or defuse. The same move is repeated over and over until it feels just right; that is, when there's an internal knowing of coordinated muscle memory and perceptual alacrity. For mastery, it's important to establish neural pathways that fire automatically for both strategy and execution of offensive and defensive abilities. All responses must become reflexive and ultimately intuitive. I apply three essential principles to achieve this: neutralizing, spiraling, and centerline. These techniques are associated with the forms of T'ai Chi, Bagua, and Hsing-I, respectively.

These are difficult techniques to explain because they really need to be experienced to fully grasp their significance. I feel it's important to talk about them, even though they seem intellectually dense. Describing them in words tends to be unwieldy. Nonetheless, these are core principles in the process of becoming invisible with No Sword.

Neutralizing an opponent is the goal of T'ai Chi. When a person strikes at you, the idea is not to meet force with force. When facing the opponent, you hold a solid stance, firmly rooted in the *dantian* (in Chinese Medicine, this is an energy center corresponding to the yogic second chakra), so that you can shift and move in a such a way to deflect their blow by not matching their strike force and using their own momentum against them. This is called receiving their energy. The resultant imbalance is used to throw them. A helpful metaphor is to envision a bear who has a solid connection to the earth. During a skirmish, the animal is quite nimble in their ability to bend or twist their body with ease.

Spiraling energy is practiced in Bagua. This martial art teaches you how to move in circles around your opponent. When walking in a circular pattern, your hips stay on the circle's outline while the upper body twists inward toward the center. This creates torsion, a mini vortex, that sends energy up through the spine in a spiraling motion. This is similar to the principle of neutralizing; however, the effect is amplified, still directing the energy away and receiving it. The spiraling is a continuous whirl around the opponent, like a relentless nipping dog darting in and retreating just enough to find a new line of attack. Bottom line: neutralizing is used against a direct punch while spiraling moves to the side of the punch.

With Hsing-I, the principle of centerline is key, which is honing the skill of exploiting the shortest and most direct path along which to attack and defend. Identifying the centerline allows you to maintain a leveraged position, making it more difficult for your opponent to control your balance and easier for you to destabilize theirs. As such, blocks are not needed. Usually in a fight, especially with a sword, whoever controls the centerline will win the match. Many charging animals do this, such as bull moose who sprints forward with directed, unyielding, lethal Power.

Neutralizing, spiraling, and centerline are classic martial arts skills that I learned over the years by studying with many teachers. I did not bestow my attention exclusively with any one school or teacher; I always looked for any information or experience, from any source, that would help me hone these important principles. As much as the prevailing structures served me to set the foundation of my martial skills, I was cautious and suspicious of any dogmatic leanings. I just could not be bound to any one way or prescribed regular form. I knew when I started to feel boxed in by any viewpoint, it was time to move on. I trusted my gut. I trusted the One to prompt and inspire me.

My aversion to capitulating to any stifling formula led me to an important understanding. When I allowed myself to be guided by my yearnings for autonomy and intrigue, I could integrate and then transcend what I'd cumulatively learned. Then I could eliminate or surpass known boundaries. Radical Freedom allowed me to integrate, transcend, and surpass. To me, Radical Freedom is a state of being where discipline and form congeal and then dissolve.

The concept of Radical Freedom is really nothing new. Innovators throughout the centuries, whether it be in science, religion, the arts, or entertainment, pushed the boundaries of existing structures. They were inspired—or perhaps had visions—to explore outside of accepted norms. I suspect they were emotionally, mentally, or spiritually stirred in some way to yank at the coattails of the establishment. In Ancient Greece, Pythagoras proposed the Earth was round. Martin Luther seeded the Reformation. Isaac Newton discerned laws of gravity and motion. The list of pioneers goes on and on: Galileo, Leonardo da Vinci, Benjamin Franklin, Thomas Edison, Albert Einstein, Marie Curie, Walt Disney, Steve Jobs, Anna Wintour, Oprah Winfrey. These people were (and are) explorers who defied convention.

Many of these exemplars have been recognized in history books for their revolutionary innovations which changed the trajectory of humankind. Some have earned cultural recognition because of their impact over many years or decades. Often, the twists and turns of their unique backstories are less known (and most likely influenced their choices). Sometimes there are mysterious circumstances that become part of a mythos and enduring legacy. It seems that with spiritual innovation, the tales and situations are more enigmatic or inexplicable, such as with Buddha and the Bodhi Tree of awakening, Moses receiving the Ten Commandments on Mount Sinai, and Krishnamacharya, the father of modern yoga, who received groundbreaking knowledge at the foot of a cave.

Martial arts are no different. Historically, fighting systems date back thousands of years, used to meet the defensive needs of hunters and warriors. Each codified approach got refined and expanded over time through the impetus of innovators who added to the existing body of knowledge and proven techniques. Students brought forth something fresh or novel by revising, reframing, and updating the conventions of their teachers. In essence, Radical Freedom captures this evolutionary approach where an innovator takes hold of the reins of progress, despite any pushback from critics and naysayers.

My experience with Radical Freedom is rooted in my longstanding connection to Taoism, Zen Buddhism, and shamanism. When I'm inspired to reach beyond my current skillset, there's a tension of sorts—a seeing, a feeling, and a knowing—that gets informed by the essential elements of each of my learned and practiced fields of study. I naturally draw from and integrate my own building blocks, like a tributary stream mixing into its larger river. I become earnestly open and acutely sensitive to the influence of Taoist flow, of Zen presence and simplicity, while shamanically connecting to some form of spirit or energy beyond me. Moreover, I connect to the One and allow the generous, present moment to unfold and rouse me. This is when I can eliminate or surpass any learned experience or known boundary. This is when discipline and form congeal and then—while in a state of non-ordinary reality—dissolve into a potent experience of Radical Freedom.

KOAN 3: SWORD OF NO SWORD

As I've mentioned before, for me, there is something mystical about the sword. When I place a sword in my hand, the weapon has a presence. It is not inert. It is not lifeless. Rather, I feel its vitality. When I spar, it emanates an active, vibrant essence, as if the weapon has a spirit or soul of its own. Sparring allows me to directly connect to this spirit.

Perhaps some of what I'm connecting to is the historical lineage and lore of sword enthusiasts throughout time who had both personal and spiritual connections to the meticulously crafted steel. The concept of spirit residing in the sword itself, as though it has been imbued with a distinctive personality and mission, has been acknowledged by historians. Perhaps the most legendary example is of King Arthur and the sword Excalibur: whoever possessed the sword was imbued with mythological Power and invincibility. The Polynesian Māori believed a weapon contained a spiritual force called *mana* and that the weapon held the spirits of its maker and all its prior owners. The Vikings named each of their Ulfberht swords and had runes inscribed on the blade as sigils for strength and to blunt an enemy's weapon during combat. The Japanese samurai with their iconic curved katana believed the soul of the weapon would possess them, thus absolving them of the violence the sword executed and clearing them of any Buddhist karmic residue.

My early attraction to weapons is somewhat inexplicable; however, I suspect I have many past life connections to them. This is especially true with medieval Spain. In junior high school I was fascinated by heroic legends such as *The Song of Roland*, the epic poem during the reign of Charlemagne; *Beowulf*, set in pagan

Scandinavia; and *Nibelungenlied*, the Germanic story of a man proving himself as a knight around 1200 CE. When I read *The Song of El Cid*, the classic medieval story of knightly honor and the glory of Spain written around 1000 CE, I felt an uncanny resonance, a connection. In the story of recapturing the northern part of Spain from the Moors, I could clearly see the battle, as if I was either El Cid himself or one of his people in the campaign who entered the newly conquered city of Toledo, the capital.

At first, I thought this could just be a young boy's fantasy. However, I had a remarkable flashback experience as an adult during my first visit there in 2004. My family and I were staying in Madrid, so we hired a driver to take us to Toledo, a city that retains many of the Roman structures since the Moors built it in the early 700s CE, including the encircling fortifying stone wall.

When we approached the entrance, I asked the driver, "Is this the main gate to the city?"

He told us, "It is the main entryway for vehicles, but the old main gate is located on the other side."

I sensed we needed to go there. So, I asked the driver to take us around, which he did. We parked the car and made our approach to what is called the Puerta de Bisagra (hinged door). This chamber-style gateway was a common design in medieval Moorish town fortifications and castles because it served as a trap, a linked passageway between two walls that is easily defended.

I knew. I knew this was *the* gate. It was the gate through which I entered with El Cid in 1081 CE.

Toledo is known as the City of the Three Cultures, because of the influences of Christians, Arabs, and Jews. It was built in the Moorish style as a maze to confuse invaders. Once you enter the main gate, there's a wall. After making a choice to go left or right, you are soon challenged by yet another wall, followed by another, and another, and so on. This way or that way? To get to the main way, you have to navigate the labyrinth. I was neither frustrated nor confused by this. I knew which way to go because it was familiar. I had lived there before. Our guide was impressed that I had the confidence and knowledge to lead us through the maze.

On another trip to Toledo with my son David in 2005, I asked our guide if he knew of any stores that sold swords. There were many because the city has been known as a traditional sword-making and metal-working center since the Roman period. When we entered the store he recommended, I could tell right away this place was not for me. It was a large space with a touristy vibe, countless display cases, cheaply made swords mounted on the walls, and many salespeople. I did see a couple of interesting swords toward the back, so I asked about them. In a short conversation with the owner, he told me they were made by one of the few remaining traditional smiths in Toledo who made the swords for the bullfights, the *estoques de torero,* and he gave me the address where I could find this man. We went there right away.

The smith's shop was far away from all the vacationers. It was a small, cozy shop, not sales-oriented, with just a few swords hung on the wall and a few in a cabinet display case. A short, older man was behind the counter, donning a leather apron as if he just stepped out of a workshop.

Since I don't speak Spanish, my son David served as my translator. He said, "We've heard you craft bullfighting blades."

Proudly, the smith took them out of the display case and showed them to us.

I then asked (with David translating), "Where are the real swords?"

The man looked quizzically at me, sizing me up, as he and David continued their exchange. He then went into the back room for a short time and brought out three other swords: a medium straight blade; a large, curved sword, made to use when straddling a horse; and a large two-handed model of a Japanese samurai sword.

These were the real thing, as I could see the properties of the steel and the characteristic metal wire wrapped handles of quality blades. Toledo steel is renowned for its durability because the blade is enveloped in a wrought iron strip, thus preventing bending or cracking. As such, these weapons are said to have a soul of iron. Also, they have a distinctive ladder or rose-like pattern on the blade with banding and mottling evocative of flowing water. Not only are such blades reputed to be shatter resistant, they can also be honed to an extremely sharp and pliant edge. With this forging process, the steel has both elasticity and hardness, yielding superior strength and maneuverability. After Hannibal used them in the Punic Wars (c. 181 BCE), Toledo steel became a standard source of weaponry for the Roman legions.

When I placed the swords in my hands, I felt the instant connection I have when I hold—or perhaps steward—such weapons. They moved me. I suspect this is the same feeling an accomplished musician gets when they are paired with a quality instrument.

I gestured to the smith, "Will you let me take them for a test drive outside in the plaza?"

With a nod, he agreed.

I instantly clicked into Radical Freedom mode, performing a freestyle combination of swinging, slashing, stabbing, and thrusting. With the speed and angle I used to cut through the air, the sword whistled as I literally danced about. David didn't miss a beat when we switched out the sword-in-hand by simultaneously throwing them to each other like a choreographed movie stunt, a skill I taught him in his younger years. A crowd gathered—surely intrigued—while the shopkeeper stood at the doorway to witness my somewhat brazen and flamboyant display. I'm sure most days he didn't experience such a demonstration. I think he was delighted.

When I stopped, we smiled at each other with a bond of kinship. He then took us back through the store to another building, which was his factory workshop. He gave us a tour and we met his entire staff. That day I purchased two of his handcrafted swords. I since have visited him twice more and we have stayed in email contact. I now own a total of four of his swords. It was such a fun adventure.

My explorations with weapons and the sword have been deeply satisfying to me. My intention was never to use my knowledge and skills as tools for hostility or cruelty. I'm fascinated by expert control and how fine weapons are crafted and used in historical and cultural contexts, such as with my adventures in Toledo. My initial pull toward martial arts was as a constructive outlet. I needed to find ways for taming and transcending my own aggressive nature. Surely, I was impacted by some poor examples of adults coping with life stressors in unhealthy ways. I witnessed many martial arts masters devolve and die young because of overindulgence and addiction to drinking, drugs, food, and sex. I worked with experts who assuredly knew their craft, yet they were way out of balance. That path was not for me; neither my upbringing nor my internal compass would allow for it.

Swords and soldiers. Fighting and combat. These topics intrigued me. But by themselves, there is no balance. Medieval knights, Japanese samurai, and Taoist and Chinese warrior monks had spiritual callings and codes of conduct. Was I a warrior? In this life, I have been training as one but not exclusively. Time and again, I have been shown by the Souls to use my skills for healing. Also, I have pursued the path of a mystic—connecting to the One.

From an early age, I was drawn toward self-development practices and spiritual ways of being in the world. I had no idea through my life choices I would keep steering myself toward developing the sensitivities of a mystic. I was fortunate to find meditation and the transcendental allure of internal martial arts as ways to maintain my equilibrium. When I was in my teens and early twenties, I did not have a vision of combining martial skills with healing arts to help others. As my life unfolded with my interests in acupuncture, Zen studies, counseling, psychology, and shamanic practices, I carried my weapons knowledge and the frameworks of my martial arts experiences forward. I integrated my aptitudes. This is how I approached my doctoral studies.

I heard about an accredited university-without-walls program from an acupuncturist colleague of mine who had completed his doctorate at the school. At the Union Institute, I was able to design my own course of studies with the guidance of a committee of mentors. They were fascinated by my premise of combining acupuncture with transpersonal psychology and shamanic practices. I explored psychiatrist Stanislav Grof's holotropic breathwork model and the spiritual and transcendent aspects of the human experience as championed by psychologist Charles Tart. My research supported the premise that acupuncture induces a deep, trance-like relaxation to lessen the sensory barrier between the conscious and unconscious mind. I was eager to expand upon my understandings of acupuncture, the field I had been working in for over ten years at the time, to show how this form of Chinese medicine could induce the non-ordinary state of consciousness needed for meaningful shamanic work while journeying with drums.

After I completed the program, the university invited me back to design and facilitate a weeklong thematic seminar. Then I was hired by a few high-tech firms to lead teambuilding retreats. Aside from getting centered through body-mind activities such as yoga and meditation, I led participants, ranging in age from early twenties to mid-sixties, through exercises aimed at facing and overcoming their fears. Through ground initiatives, team members would rely on each other to solve problems outside in nature and on a high ropes course. I anticipated that physical challenges with unfamiliar equipment dangling in the trees would most likely emotionally stir or even trigger folks so as to bond team members during crisis situations.

Also at these retreats, I led drills with wooden Japanese swords, called *bokken*, teaching basic swings and steps. I was excited to use my martial arts skills in a context for the personal growth and healing of others. Without doubt, most people are afraid of the sword, initially perceiving it as an intimidating, primitive weapon, as it is often associated with unrestrained aggression. Few have any experience with defensive blades or the skillset to manage what could be seen as a menacing armament. My crafted intention was to push emotional limits in a supportive environment where we could look at how we respond to prompts and stressors that are outside of our comfort zones.

On the last day, we suited up in body armor and each participant had to spar with me for a minute or two. I recall one guy, Dave, from Washington, D.C., who was an active-duty officer in the Green Berets. He was an asset to me and the teams as an experienced leader with a competitive edge who knew how to organize and inspire people. During the one-on-one swordplay, he was determined to take me down, so I used a standard defensive position with my sword held out in front of me, pointed at his face. Dave was resolute. He wanted to hit me. To do so, he would have to find a way to move inside the point of my sword to reach me. Of course, we were donning protective masks with full body armor, so neither of us would get hurt. Every time he took a step toward me, I would poke him in the face, in a fun-loving yet provocative way, which both annoyed and frustrated him. Dave was a good sport. Eventually, he became exhausted and gave up. We both had a great laugh and ended our match with a big hug.

I've taken great pleasure in training students at all levels with the sword. With each encounter, I always learn something about human nature, how each student has a complex, nuanced way of approaching the world. I rise to the challenge of finding ways to facilitate growth while pushing my clients out of their comfort zones so they can discover their innate gifts and strengths.

As I honed my own sword skills, I delighted in working with my advanced students because they challenged me to push beyond my own limits. This is how I refined the concept of *winding*. This sword technique, derived from the German school of fencing, is rooted in a move called *Krumphau* (crooked-hew). This is because the sword stroke is a vertical slash that reaches across the center line to the opponent, traveling left from a right position and vice versa. This move is considered a master-level feat because it likely originated as a stealthy strategy, requiring a full grasp of the aforementioned foundational techniques of neutralizing, spiraling, and centerline.

The challenge of winding is to integrate several key principles: deflecting the opponent's energy away from you or absorbing it and sending it back to them; not meeting force with force; and keenly holding awareness of the challenger's energetic paths and patterns of attack. Winding requires an intensity of perception to connect to the opponent's sword through a lens of unyielding, sharp discernment, much like my experiences where Brother Hawk and I merged when hunting.

With my advanced students, winding is our initial movement as sword partners, which then transitions into sparring. An observer would probably see the encounter as not-so-interesting, repetitive, dance-like, circular, and full of figure-eight motions. Conceptually, winding mimics the movements used in T'ai Chi push hands, a technique that is used to check posture, alignment, internal and external strength, stepping, weight shifts, and balance. The internal focus of push hands trains the practitioner to become an active listener with the body, connecting, assessing, and flowing. These skills are imperative refinements for achieving martial arts mastery and are not exclusive to any offensive or defensive technique. Similarly, for example, Capoeira—the Brazilian martial art that combines elements of dance and complex acrobatic-like maneuvers—uses a fundamental footwork called *ginga* that involves rocking back and forth to connect to the opponent's energy.

I used winding as a foundational construct, greatly expanding it through years of trial and error, as a way to enter the shamanic Realms. I realized that at some point when your opponent attacks and you wind or blend with them, there is brief time when your sword "disappears" to your challenger. They get unbalanced physically or mentally, thus creating an opening. How? Simply put: I surrender. When my challenger strikes, I yield to the energic wave and ride it. This confuses the opponent because, despite their calculated resolve, they no longer are in control and don't know what's happening. In that flicker of a moment when their purposeful determination couples with their willful, anticipated takedown, they are taken aback. Surprised, they become vulnerable and defenseless.

The same principle is used in some contact sports and other martial arts, such as in wrestling or grappling, Judo, Aikido, or T'ai Chi. Basically, it's physics. In T'ai Chi, we talk about issuing energy, which takes into account potential and kinetic energy. Since energy is always in motion and always shifting between potential and kinetic, practicing and perfecting the transference of these energies creates a combined skillful eye and kinesthetic sense that can both manage and harness their flow to one's advantage.

In Aikido, one the most fundamental yet unique techniques is *irimi nage*, which literally means "enter and throw." The defender connects with the attacker's forward thrust, absorbs their energy, and fluidly continues its course with the addition of their own energy to impel the attacker off balance. In essence, I blend and move with my partner. When sparring with a sword, the attacker discovers they're caught in an instant of disbelief because their weapon is not where they intended. They then fall into a seeming abyss—a gap in time—where they struggle with their placement and orientation. As they attempt to catch themselves, it's too late to recover from being ensnared in my ploy. Game over. If we were not playing, per se, they'd be left exposed and subjected to defeat by a deadly blow.

My students often describe the ineffable moment when the sword disappears as "an energetic illusion that can be used as a transport portal to other Realms." Indeed, it is a strange and extraordinary phenomenon. Even though they are moving quickly, to the swordsman, time seems to slow. And if you can identify that temporal shift and yield to it, you can cross a threshold beyond the present boundary of space-time to pierce the veil

KOAN 3: SWORD OF NO SWORD 113

into what shamanic practitioners would call non-ordinary reality. This may sound farfetched, but this concept is colloquially referred to as 'being in the zone', the immersive state of an energized focus of full involvement, resulting in the transformation of one's sense of time. This mental state is explained through the lens of positive psychology as *flow state*.

As a form of hyperfocus in sports, athletes speak of their moments in the zone when the game slows—or sometimes freezes—and they get clarity and vision for tracking the ball or making the winning move. Writers recount immersive blocks of time when hours of inspired composition pass seamlessly. Musicians describe riding notes, vibrations, and phrases, pulling them from their awareness of the concert venue into altered consciousness during performances.

Flow state is often achieved during spiritual practices, such as with Raja yoga and the practice of Samyama, an all-embracing, focused concentration during meditation resulting in divine union. Ecstatic trance dance dates back to antiquity and are found, for example, in Balinese ritual dance, Santeria, Sufi whirling, worldwide shamanic traditions, ancestral tributes, pagan witchcraft, and modern Wicca. Zen monks in India and China have been achieving extended states of focus during meditation for centuries.

Perhaps my Zen training provided the foundation for me to integrate hyperfocus and the ensuing flow state into my martial arts training. I initially used winding to cultivate and harness Power to defeat my opponent. The principles involved with winding blend all the skills I learned with spiraling, neutralizing, and centerline through many years of practice while braving countless encounters of trial and error. Winding requires putting into action an intricate skillset of receiving and deflecting energy plus attention to pathways for attacking and defending. It's a delightful puzzler where I'm engaging my body and mind to be in sharp accord. But I did not expect winding to present itself as a doorway to shamanic Realms.

One day, while sparring outside with John and Mike, I looked up and saw a break in the canopy between two rows of large pine trees. In that space where the clear blue sky splayed its familiar expansive background, Ueshiba (1883–1969)—the Japanese martial artist and founder of Aikido—appeared to me. I knew it was him because I had seen his picture many times over the years during my studies. I wasn't surprised to encounter a long-passed soul because I actively call energies to me for guidance, especially with my shamanic workings.

> *I wield my sword. I call the souls. "O-Sensei" (the honorific title for Ueshiba) appears. This is not unusual, as he has been visiting me for almost a year. We merge. I ask him, "How do I disappear by using my sword?" He beckons me to strike at him.*
>
> *He shows me, in slow motion, what to do. I recognize the move. It is irimi nage. It is more, though. His energy, so quiet and peaceful, reaches out to me.*
>
> *It feels like I am in the center of a hurricane.*
>
> *He draws me to him. His energy pulls me toward him. I am totally in his control. He gets me off balance when he turns. Then he blends with me. At that moment, O-Sensei disappears.*
>
> *I feel Power all around, yet it is still peaceful in the center of the hurricane.*
>
> *I know he is still there with me. We hold the space together. So peaceful. Then he moves, breaking the bond. I fall forward but stay on my feet.*

He has not yet left. I ask him more about the move.
He walks toward me. So calm but so intense.
He moves in front of me, a few feet away.
We are still in the center of the hurricane.
The world has disappeared. It is just the two of us, together. Calm. All around us is a hurricane powered by him.
He disappears yet is still there. I feel him.
We stay there for what seems like eternity.
Then he moves away. The hurricane dissipates. He is gone.
Now I understand the energy and dynamics of disappearing with the sword.

I found it remarkable to have contact with Ueshiba since I never studied Aikido. I do hold him in high regard as one of the greatest warriors of the twentieth century. Maybe it wasn't Ueshiba—it is possible I called the attention of another soul with similar energies and skillset. In any case, there was a definite transcendence of the moment from ordinary to non-ordinary reality while I was winding with John:

The Power builds to such a frequency that it feels like an explosive pop where time and space suspend.

In this kind of moment, which is difficult to describe or know exactly how long it lasts, my keen sense of seeing and feeling confirms a knowing that what I perceive is genuine.

All at once, my body is moving, yet frozen in time. My mind is actively engaged in the sparring yet boosted to receive a distinctive communication with a download of ethereal knowledge.

Some of it makes sense immediately. Some of it is revealed later, like a time-release tablet, yet I recognized its original source.

From this day forward, I will be able to call upon Ueshiba at will, similar to opening a website I've visited before where the browser has cached the address and seamlessly pulls up the visuals and information.

Another master swordsman, Tesshū, informed my practice, in a very a different way than Ueshiba. I read extensively about this great warrior and statesman, Yamaoka Tesshū (1836–1888), though I never connected to him in the Realms, as I did with Ueshiba. Yet I could both see and feel him. His energy was the archetype I worked conscientiously to stay away from. In many ways, he represented the angry and violent temperament of myself as a youth, a suffering I'd sought to transcend. And he typified the type of martial arts teachers I'd experienced and decided to avoid.

He kept building his yang energy without seeking a counterbalance. It is said he had to drink lots of sake every day to calm the Power he had accumulated. Also, he was known for working his students to exhaustion as a technique to achieve connection to non-ordinary reality. For example, he would instruct them to perform one thousand sword strikes to push the limits of one's mental and physical capacity.

Yet he asserted and taught in his school two astounding beliefs: the perceived discrepancy between the sword and the self is illusory and the perceived discrepancy between oneself and one's opponent is illusory. I learned from Tesshū that with practice, I could merge with the sword and with my opponent in an interconnected state of Oneness.

This concept is extraordinary for swordsmanship, requiring years of training to attain. And at the same time, it was nothing new to me. My Taoist and Zen studies always supported an underlying tenet of coherence. As a mystic, my daily practice was to connect to the One. Through swordplay, I challenged myself to attain the same—or at least a similar—connection to the One. The gift was an amazing discovery: through sparring, I could cultivate Power and be transported to other Realms. In that process, my energy shifted in such a way that I melded with the energetic matrix.

Ueshiba and Tesshū—two of the most influential "mentors" I've encountered on my journey to understanding how to use the sword as a tool for accessing the Realms—exemplify the contrast of the hard and soft approaches to martial arts. They represent the yin and yang, both holding valuable lessons, just with different approaches that yield complementary yet contrasting results. Combined with my practice and learnings from Munenori about mushin, I have achieved a unique bridge for connecting to the One when sparring with the sword.

I can imagine sitting in a room and chatting with these three prominent teachers. They would coach me with exacting words:

Observe one thing. Discern everything. Witness your opponent before you. Notice the periphery. Hyperfocus. Soft focus. Park your mind here. Be in the Realms. Merge with the sword. Be now here. Perceive the energy. See. Feel. Be the energy. Know. Let go. Allow.

Those instructions would repeat in an endless loop, like a recorded message beaming from a control tower, until they fused with my consciousness so that I was seamlessly operating, as if on autopilot. The words of my teachers build my confidence even to this day. I trust my judgment and experience for what seems like blindly navigating a ship into a foggy abyss. I've learned to trust the partnership of myself and a host of helping spirits. Ultimately, my teachers have showed me how to cultivate Power—to imbue and direct energy with intention.

When sparring I give way to all my understandings about the control of the weapon. Then I surrender. It is Radical Freedom, where all the structures I've discovered and gathered for my body and mind to handle can now be cast to the wind, like a tree naturally shedding its leaves from a potent gust. I am now liberated to solve the puzzle at hand by transcending my known structures. The Radical Freedom approach both eliminates and surpasses any learned experience or known boundaries. It's freeing. I'm riding a flow of energy. And I am the flow.

The sword is my guide. I use it as a gateway to the Realms:

There is Power here. There is Power there. Why is that so?

Because it's definitively genuine. There's authenticity, both curated and raw. My expression of Radical Freedom is a confluence of what resonates with how I have modelled my life and defined my being.

How so? My warrior spirit surges. There's physicality. There's skill and strategy applied through martial arts. There's Taoist and Zen philosophies coloring all my perceptions. There's single-minded exuberance and serious focus. It's stoic. It's gritty. It's both empty and full. It's crystal clear. And vague. It's a muddle of chaos and order. I accept all that it is. I accede to what it is not. I channel all these elements into accessing the One through a portal of surrender so I can solve the koan of the moment.

I am in a convergent zone. I am both here and there and nowhere, fully immersed in a transcendent spiritual journey. I am one with the timeless moment itself, of what is most real, most true, right here and right now.

It is both tactical and unrelated to the sparring at hand. I commingle with the ineffable where I am open to any way of being that is outside my ordinary experience of this earthly reality. Time slows and sometimes stills. In that freeze frame, often there are profound insights and musings.

And not. Sometimes it is purely a mystical, mysterious, magical moment—or an indeterminate series of moments.

This is one expression of my Power. This is me in my Power. This is me as Power.

I am deeply honored to have known my mentors. The path at times was arduous. Sometimes I stumbled and screwed up. Many trained me by modeling their essence. I hold deep, heartfelt gratitude for their guidance—those who walked this Earth with me and those whom I encountered in the Realms. Through their wisdom—much of it received via energetic transmissions—I can revisit this wondrous state of non-ordinary reality, time and again.

I am blessed.

QUESTIONS FOR SELF-REFLECTION

- How do you connect to the One? . . . through dancing, painting, singing, writing, swordplay?

- What is your Way?

- How can you engage your body-mind to connect to the One during your activities and pursuits?

KOAN 4

It's a little past dawn now and I haven't slept. Sun rays are peering through the window. I am in my hospital bed. Severe pain. My lower back, throbbing. My legs, won't move. My feet, on fire. My mind, racing: How did I get to this point?

I look up. The orthopedic surgeon is standing at the foot of the bed in a nice leather jacket. He is going to Bermuda, he tells me. He takes hold of my big toes. A squeeze.

"Can you feel this?"

I nod my head.

"Thank goodness for that." He's caring. And stoic. "The next two weeks will be torture."

This is good news, considering.

"But then the pain will lessen."

I stare ahead. "Sounds like fun."

He nods. Looks me in the eye. Walks out of the room. Stillness. I am left behind to fulfill his prophecy about the pain.

Threshhold Guardian

I've always had problems with my back. It seems to run in the family—my father, my brother, my sister. None of them ended up needing surgery on the lumbar area as I did, although my younger brother had an operation on his cervical vertebrae.

The first omen appeared when I was on a family vacation in Spain in 2000. We love traveling to places rich in history. This trip, to Córdoba, was not a pilgrimage, yet it felt like a soulful journey because I'm such a history buff and I'm attracted to spiritual places. When we travel overseas, we often mix it up between guided tours and exploring on our own. I loved wandering through all the narrow, winding streets, passing by many of the renowned jewelers, silversmiths, and watchmakers.

Córdoba is the birthplace of the Roman philosopher Seneca (c. 4 BCE–65 CE), who is recognized as one the famous stoics. In a letter written to his friend Lucilius, an official of Ancient Rome living in Sicily at the time, Seneca advised prioritizing mental development over physical training: "Pray for a sound mind and good health, first of soul and then of body." His words somewhat foreshadow my struggles, as I would need to emphasize my inner resources to overcome many physical limitations as they unfurled in the years to come.

We just finished touring the Great Mosque, known locally as Mezquite Cathedral. It is one of the oldest structures in the city still standing from the late eighth century. The building itself has a long, complex story of reconstruction and repurposing. Historians believe there had been a temple honoring the god Janus on the site during the Roman Empire. That temple was converted into a church dedicated to Saint Vincent by the invading Visigoths in 572 CE. Then the church was converted into an Islamic mosque by the Umayyad Caliphate and completely rebuilt in 785 CE. In 1236, it was converted into a Catholic cathedral by Ferdinand III and dedicated to the Virgin Mary. My fascination with this historical site came to an abrupt halt when I felt a sharp, stabbing pain in my lower back, radiating into my groin and upper femur.

At first, I thought it was a hip problem. I know it sounds silly, but as a martial arts person, I am keenly aware of my body so I can perform intricate moves on demand, but I also have learned not to listen to my body. I know pain is a messenger. I use pain as energy, too, as a way to fuel additional Power to push through. Of course, when there's extreme pain, you have to stop. That's the peculiar rub any serious athlete knows about. Where is that edge? How much should I press on before I exhaust or damage my body?

This time, I pressed on. I saw no reason not to continue. I didn't stop our sightseeing. We didn't return to the hotel. I acknowledged the pain and figured if I could get the muscles to relax, I'd be just fine. After a few stretches, I could tell from how my body responded, this time was surely different. Something was amiss, yet I treated it like any other overuse injury. I defaulted to my experience and training as a martial artist on what to do.

The first approach for nursing most sports injuries is RICE: rest, ice, compression, and elevation. This was of little help. RICE is usually applied as a triage of sorts for a fresh injury. I knew this treatment might only be a temporary fix but doing so would help me determine the next steps, if need be.

Once we returned home, I was set on proactively addressing any skeleto-muscular imbalances. I scheduled bodywork massages and acupuncture sessions. I hired a personal trainer and physical therapist. I stretched daily with yoga and committed to a weight resistance strengthening routine. I was determined to manage what I regarded as age-appropriate wear-and-tear on my body. After all, I pounded on my body in my teens playing football and lacrosse. Then I stressed my joints and connective tissues with punches and kicks and swordplay while immersed in years of martial arts training from my twenties and into my fifties.

I was used to pushing the physical limits of my body and I had trained my mind to recognize distractions and deal with them head on. I trained. I stayed on task. I kept focus. That's me. Strong-willed and robust. I was determined to push through this injury, as warriors do, because this was not really a crisis—yet.

That changed in February 2007, when the obscure omen from the trip to Córdoba came to light. We were renovating our home, which required us to vacate so the infrastructure could be upgraded. The entire team was on site: the architect, general contractor, kitchen designer, and construction supervisor. There were temporary windows in the house and the heat was turned off in the building, so the bitter New England cold followed us inside. All the furniture had been removed. There was no place to sit.

After standing the whole morning for the meeting, we went to lunch at one of my favorite Asian fusion restaurants, Blue Ginger, because it was known in part for its allergen-free dining options, including gluten-free and dairy-free dishes. Then, while seated, I noticed a strange sensation in my left foot. It was numb. Most likely, I thought, my body is reacting to being in the chilly house for a long time. I figured the numbness would just work itself out. It didn't. Rather, the sensation intensified, like the peculiar tingling and swollen feeling after a Novocain injection at the dentist. I hobbled out of the restaurant, concerned for my well-being and with the tenacity to find out what was awry in my body. Now there was an urgency.

Eventually, I could not dorsiflex the foot, which means that when walking, I couldn't raise my toes upward as the foot came up off the ground to take the next step. This was serious. At my next visit with my physical therapist, an orthopedist and chiropractor came to assess me. They all observed my gait. Immediate diagnosis: foot drop. Not good. The focus now was on my spine. The most common cause of foot drop is peroneal nerve injury. The peroneal nerve is a branch of the sciatic nerve that supplies movement and sensation to the lower leg, foot, and toes. An MRI would confirm their opinion.

As a lifelong martial artist, this circumstance was a hard blow to both my self-esteem and my body. I worked so hard—for most of my life—to hone the tactical and kinesthetic skills needed to be at the top of my game. *Emasculation.* This prognosis cut at the core of my being as an archetypal warrior who trained his body and mind attentively and diligently. In hindsight, I'm somewhat astounded by my stubborn resolve, because with all the ups and downs of the physical setbacks and pain, I had already endured years of somatic and emotional turmoil while this condition not-so-quietly festered. Now this.

I live with warrior energy. I've always been that way. I hold steady through adversity with resolute commitment. I don't back down. I continually assess situations strategically. I don't show signs of weakness because that kind of vulnerability—especially for a warrior—could be fatal. I've been this way for as long as I can remember. The warrior energy in me is what my shamanic teacher, Natasha, could see in the Realms. It is how she called me to her through the dream that led to our fateful meeting and changed the course of my life.

In 2003, just a few years before the unfolding of my spinal enigma, I had a peculiar experience inside a European church. It was a confirmation, of sorts, of my lifelong draw toward the warrior energy. We were in Paris, on the left bank of the Seine in Saint-Germain-des-Prés. This historical section is currently famous for its bohemian spirit and known for its literary and artistic legacy of nineteenth-century writers and artists, including Hemingway, Fitzgerald, Sartre, Monet, and Picasso. Tourists love the quarter for its cafes, bars, restaurants, and boutique shopping. In the Middle Ages, Saint-Germain-des-Prés was both a religious and cultural center, with a church and abbey, built in 558 AD, prominently situated in what was at the time fields and meadows—or *prés*—located outside the walls of medieval Paris.

It was August. Even with the heavy, hot air, the streets were bustling with tourists. To get away from the crowds, I sought refuge and solace at the church. Unlike Notre Dame and other cathedrals I've seen, the exterior stonework felt rather weighty, more mundane, with the interior decor less ornate although still quite impressive. I entered the large building and found a seat toward the back. There were no pews; rather, rows and rows of simple wooden chairs filled the great hall. It was cool, quiet, and somewhat dark compared to the brilliant outdoor sunlight. For me, it was a perfect respite. A priest, or perhaps a monk, kept a watchful yet respectful eye on those who entered. I think he figured I was praying since my eyes were closed intently and I'm sure I was holding reverent energy. I was deep in meditation, settling into stillness.

Then, I heard a voice behind me. "Welcome, Christian soldier." I opened my eyes and looked all around. The church was empty except for the observant cleric. No matter. It was probably the busyness of my mind settling in to the quiet. I continued meditating.

Again, I heard, firmly asserted, "Welcome, Christian soldier." I opened my eyes, this time to an image. I saw a man wearing a white smock with a layer of chainmail armor underneath. Around his neck was a leather cord affixed to a black cross. At his waist, a long sword was attached to his belt. He had no helmet. Immediately, I knew I was seeing the spirit of Saint Germain. I had no doubt it was him.

I spoke back. "You are wrong, sir. I am not a Christian soldier. I'm not even Christian."

He smiled self-assuredly and replied, "What you are now is of no importance. You are one of my Christian soldiers." Then he vanished.

I received his words initially with curiosity and then with a clear sense of knowing. In another time, I was one of his soldiers. Then I recalled that Saint Germain was a great knight who was instrumental in converting many "barbarian tribes" to Christianity, which he considered to be the true faith. In that time, I did his bidding.

This validation from such a notable figure may have been one more hint at why I resonated deeply with the warrior ideal. Often, I'm told I personify warrior traits such as confidence, strength, aggressiveness, discipline, and the relentless need to be active. I think warrior attributes have a psychic anchor in me, aside from being in my DNA.

Many years later, I realized something was amiss with my recollection. Saint Germain was not a knight. He lived from 496–576 CE, at the beginning of the medieval period, thus predating the knights. The medieval period (also called the Dark Ages or the Middle Ages) was a long one, lasting from the fifth to the fifteenth centuries. Early on, Saint Germain was an authoritative influencer for the displacement of paganism with Christianity. Much later, the feudal knights were active players in the Crusades, from 1095–1291. The seat of Templar Power was in France with the same mission, and near the same location as Saint Germain. The church where I encountered his spirit is located in the vicinity of all these historical happenings. In hindsight, I think there's an overlap of these related warrior energies.

I discovered, too, that Saint Germain as a bishop practiced the virtues and austerities of his monastic life, working to diminish the suffering caused by incessant wars. I resonate with the mission of reducing suffering for humanity, through my bodhisattva vow and through my lifelong vocation of shamanic counselling and workings. Since my experience in the Saint-Germain-des-Prés church, I often contact Saint Germain during my daily meditations. I carry forward our encounter in the church, evoking the composite of both the fervent and compassionate energies that Saint Germain represents for me.

Warriors persist, despite setbacks. Warriors push through injury with resolve. Any supposed past life experience I had as a soldier got tested when, for the seven years following my peroneal nerve injury diagnosis, I suffered through emotional and physical turmoil as both my left ankle and left leg weakened. It was a relentless volley of sorting through the muddle of both the known and unknown about what was happening inside my body. I had moments of despair. I had moments of hope. There was one unfortunate, unshakeable component in the mix—pain.

Initially, I tried a mechanical and energetic approach. Acupuncture. Yoga. Pilates. Assisted stretching. Lower spine traction to elongate the vertebrae and take pressure off the pinched nerves. An orthopedic doctor suggested I get fitted for plastic braces to bolster foot stability, one that articulated and one that didn't. These provided some relief for a short time, but they added another kind of pain through discomfort due to the way they pressed and rubbed on my leg. Also, they were bulky. They threw off my already compromised gait.

Then I tried walking with a cane. It was an imperfect solution because it created a lopsided muscular imbalance whenever I shifted most of my weight to one side for support. My Pilates instructor suggested I use forearm crutches, one for each arm. That helped. Even so, I kept falling. I tripped on carpets. I went down unexpectedly, many times when I was methodically mindful of my surroundings and body mechanics. It so frustrated me when I fell, even when I was sure of my balance in the moment.

KOAN 4: THRESHHOLD GUARDIAN

One year while I was dealing with this, one of my sons came home from college for Christmas break. Before heading back to school, he wanted to go clothes shopping. We ventured out to a huge discount mall near our home. The weather was typical for Massachusetts in early January: frigid. I didn't expect any after-Christmas bustle. Yet the place was a frenetic mob scene. The parking lot was mostly full. We kept circling for a spot closer to the entrance until we decided we had to look at the farthest end of the lot, a couple hundred yards away. Once inside, while my son made his way through many stores, I had to stop and sit several times because I was hindered by the pain. When it was time to leave, I was consumed by the pain and unable to walk the distance back to the vehicle. He had to bring the car to me. This was a tipping point. I couldn't power through. The pain finally won out.

As soon as possible, I spoke with my physician, who suggested I get a handicap placard so I could park as close as possible in most locations, when needed. I struggled with the altered image of me as a hobbling yet not-so-old man. I wasn't that concerned about how others saw me because the exterior presentation to any onlookers didn't convey the essence of the tenacious Red Dragon within me. I wasn't ready to give up nor give in to a dwindling narrative of "sword-wielding martial artist forfeits his standing and becomes a weakened, vulnerable fellow." This just wasn't the truth. My body may have been betraying me, but my mind was strong, bolstered by staunch determination. I wouldn't concede. But the reality was harsh: I couldn't walk across the room without my leg giving way. Relentless pain was now my norm. Despite my limitations, I kept pushing.

This was especially discouraging on family vacations, such as when we were in Scotland, exploring castles and traversing moors. I just couldn't keep up. It was inevitable that my mobility would take a nose-dive, since in hindsight, I can see I was treading water.

I certainly wasn't avoiding the situation with all the interventions I tried. But no approach provided relief. Realistically, I couldn't keep living that way.

The final reckoning came when we visited Wales. The country is renowned for more castles per square mile than any other country in the world. For one thousand years, it was contested territory with the Iberians, Brythons, Romans, Anglo-Saxons, and Normans. This included centuries of fighting between Welsh princes and the kings of England. Wales originally had about six hundred castles, of which over one hundred are still standing, either as ruins or as restored buildings.

We were touring Harlech Castle, built upon a rocky crag overlooking the ocean and the dunes below. Its classic "walls within walls" design creates a daunting natural defense. It is said that ships shielding the castle could moor alongside the fortress walls for the troops to be supplied and fed. A modern-day floating footbridge now provides tourists with access across the expansive moat of yore, as Castle Harlech is an architectural marvel of engineering. UNESCO has deemed it a World Heritage Site.

I remember that day, distinctly. It was a typical Sunday morning in May in Great Britain—pouring rain with wind gusts holding at thirty to forty miles per hour. In many ways, it paralleled the seasonal New England weather I'm used to. Springtime holds the promise of milder conditions, yet the cyclical transition is often less idyllic. As we climbed the stairs of the forty-foot tower, my son acted as a support from behind, catching me when my gait faltered and pushing me upward. My body struggled. This was a challenge that in years past would have posed absolutely no difficulty at all. We made it to the top, which surely was satisfying, but there were no walls or roof protecting us from the sheets of rain now coming at us horizontally.

KOAN 4: THRESHHOLD GUARDIAN

I looked toward the land, below. I could see the Royal St. David's Golf Club, where many championships have taken place throughout the years since 1894. The opening dozen holes on the fairway are fully exposed to the elements, reminding us that this day was a harsh one to golf. To my surprise, there was a long line, maybe dozens of people, waiting to play the first hole. A gust of wind whooshed hard with blinding rain. It almost blew us over, so we quickly sat down on the tower's exposed surface. When the squall abated, my son and wife stood with an urgency for us to seek cover in the indoor stairwell. I couldn't get up. I was besieged by debilitating pain. And drenched.

Time halted. At that instant, my body was immobilized and my mind reeled, penetrating my awareness beyond the pain. I went deep inside to a noiseless place of knowing. I heard my internal voice firmly assert, *I can't keep doing this. I need to accept this reality.* Just below, I watched as people teed up, not resisting the unpleasant conditions. They were persisting—choosing to suffer. This stark observation struck me as the pounding sheets of rain continued. As I peered down from a battlement atop a fortress—in distress—I had a profound insight.

There I was, my body incapacitated, strewn on a cold, wet, stony floor, with the heavens gnashing from above. I then asked, *Why are those people willingly enduring such discomfort? They could make a different choice.* I was immersed in an absurdly blaring metaphor that I would have been foolish to ignore.

Pay attention, John! I told myself. *Now what?* I asked. Then a flash of sorts from beyond me dropped a word like a bomb: *Surgery.*

Just the word terrified me. In my counseling practice, I heard so many times from countless patients how surgical procedures often didn't turn out as expected. Usually, more complications followed and resolution of the original health condition was illusory. My initial reaction to body ailments was to assess if wholistic treatment options could help. The Chinese approach—acupuncture—has its value, typically to treat pain. As a practitioner, I've facilitated and observed progress and transformations that have brought many patients relief. Now, it has become more acceptable in America for acupuncture to be used for overall wellness, including stress management.

Certainly, allopathic medicine has its strengths. A broken bone requires diagnostic imaging, immobilization, and follow-up physical therapy for it to effectively heal. An ear infection responds relatively quickly to antibiotics with few side effects. Modern treatments for heart disorders, both electrical and structural, are miraculous. The allopathic approach was signaling to me with a flashing yellow light.

I realized I was at a crossroads. I could continue down the current path, a lengthy, rutted, hilly climb. Or I could choose another track, a steep cliff with a potential freefall where I might hit the bottom in a disheveled heap. My typical reaction to traditional routes was to go in the opposite direction, as strange as that may seem. When working with my patients who are stuck, I'd discovered that when an established way—a groove—isn't working, then it makes no sense to keep doing the same thing over and over again while expecting a different result.

You have to choose, John, my inner voice badgered me. *There's no perfect, guaranteed solution.* The warrior in me wanted to fight. The healer in me implored me to be sensible. The practical adult in me warned my dogged self to carefully yield.

Back home, the whirlwind of medical diagnostics and interventions snowballed. More MRIs and x-rays. I researched the best doctors in Boston. I met with spine specialists and neurosurgeons. Diagnosis: lumbar spinal stenosis. Intervention: surgery. Scope: lumbar laminectomy, L2 through S1. Prognosis: undetermined. Complication: the spine is growing toward the nerves and their branches. The laminectomy would create space for the spinal cord by removing any bony overgrowths or interfering tissues. A successful outcome *might* mitigate muscle weakness, numbness, and pain. It was a risky procedure. I could come out worse than when I went in. I thought, *We are now in serious territory.*

What would change? Possibly everything. My outer world, as I knew it, was dissolving. The truth was, my life had been compromised for a long time. I struck a bargain with myself to accept the gradual changes with an elusive good faith that somehow resolution was afoot. But the spiritual approach was falling short. I was constantly assessing the psychic energy around the situation and looking at any Power dynamics from a shamanic perspective. I used loving energy through Ho'oponopono daily to transmute the frustration, pain, and anger. It wasn't enough.

I was a resourceful, tenacious warrior archetype who had always prevailed. I did a great job holding on. But it was time to let go because I had reached yet another dead end in this labyrinth. I had to let go of getting better, of beating the odds. I could not overcome the pain. It just wasn't possible, short of a miracle. The life I had crafted and enjoyed was finished. I had to surrender.

But the deeply entrenched warrior in me was balking. Was this resignation? Was I waving white flags, admitting defeat? No! Absolutely not. My physical health had been compromised, surely. But my mind was strong. My faith—devoid of religiosity yet intrepid in spiritual connection to the One—was my anchor. Since outward focus was no longer an option, I went deeper and deeper inside of myself. This saved my life. I surrendered to the One and trusted the Universe.

My trust in Spirit has served me well throughout my entire life. I was born in the Chinese Year of the Dragon. I definitely hold those traditional traits associated with the dragon: enthusiastic, confident, not afraid of challenges, willing to take risks, and sometimes aggressive. In the late 1970s when I was studying with my mentor Paul Gallagher, an expert in Taoism, Chinese language, and culture, he helped me integrate the teachings of the *Tao Te Ching*, the central text of Taoism. *Tao* means "way." *Te* means "power." *Ching* means "classical book." Together, this is translated as the "Way of Power." Some translate it as the "Way and Its Power." The Way is a spiritual path. Because Paul was so keen on all the classical ways of Chinese culture, all of his students took Chinese names, just for fun. Because I was born in the Year of the Dragon and my favorite color is red, I took on the name Ger Lung, which translates to "Red Dragon." That was my Way forward—the Way of the Red Dragon. To transcend the difficulties that lay ahead, I would look to a skillset I had been cultivating in this lifetime: the spiritual path of inner alchemy, shamanic Power, and the journey within.

In times of trouble, some people seek solace through prayer in solitude or inside houses of worship. Some folks immerse themselves in arts or craft projects. I know people who take to complex undertakings through painting or knitting or find their way into their garages and makeshift woodshops to tinker. To me, these are all inroads to making space for possible insight once the mind is actively occupied. The foreground busyness allows for deeper thought processes to percolate in the background.

I turned to martial arts. I took to the sword. It engaged me. It freed me. It pulled me both further in and further out. It was how

I connected to energies and communed with souls. I practiced mostly outside, so I could bond with nature, connecting to the sky and grounding with the Earth. I attuned to the vibrations of everything around me as they resonated—drifting clouds, stationary trees, swirling air, the brilliant sun. The sword directed my concentration inward, outward, above, below, beyond. It modulated from soft focus to hyperfocus. I found portals to other Realms. I followed them to novel and unknown whereabouts to listen and learn.

This was my workshop. It was where I connected with energies, souls, and ancestors. I gathered information. I experienced distortions in space and time. This was the place and space of engagement where absolutely nothing and so much happened, both in the foreground and background. For decades, it was my sanctuary. But, with the prospect of losing my strength and mobility as I knew it, I was uncertain. Would I be able to stand again? Would I hold the sword again?

March 15, 2013. Boston, Massachusetts. New England Baptist Hospital. 7:30 to 11:30 a.m. Four hours of surgery. Lumbar laminectomy: four levels, L2 through S1.

The lumbar spine makes up the lower end of the spinal column. It consists of five lumbar vertebra that are numbered 1 through 5, from top to bottom. The L5 vertebra is connected to the top of the sacrum (named the S1 segment) through an intervertebral disc. L2, L3, and L4 spinal nerves provide sensation to the front part of the thigh and inner side of the lower leg. These nerves also control hip and knee muscle movements. A lot could go wrong when surgeons work on this area. Fortunately, the procedure was successful: no complications on the operating table.

> *It's a little past dawn now and I haven't slept. Sun rays are peering through the window. I am in my hospital bed. Severe pain. My lower back, throbbing. My legs, won't move. My feet, on fire. My mind, racing: How did I get to this point?*
>
> *I look up. The orthopedic surgeon is standing at the foot of the bed in a nice leather jacket. He is going to Bermuda, he tells me. He takes hold of my big toes. A squeeze.*
>
> *"Can you feel this?"*
>
> *I nod my head.*
>
> *"Thank goodness for that." He's caring. And stoic. "The next two weeks will be torture."*
>
> *This is good news, considering.*
>
> *"But then the pain will lessen."*
>
> *I stare ahead. "Sounds like fun."*
>
> *He nods. Looks me in the eye. Walks out of the room. Stillness. I am left behind to fulfill his prophecy about the pain.*

The post-surgical pain was far beyond what I imagined. I was confident I could handle any type of discomfort, but this was beyond compare. The pain was off the charts. For the first few days, I could barely move. Still, the nurses carefully wrested my aching body out of bed for a labored stroll a couple times each day, assisted by a walker. To my surprise, the hospital stay was only a few days. Unfortunately, the pain meds made me sick. Once home, I stopped taking them and relied only on mindfulness breathing techniques.

I was in recovery at home for six weeks. I had lots of time to think and reflect. I was particularly attentive to the changes in my body because any potential post-surgical complications from a laminectomy are serious: chest infection, blood clots in the legs, or damage to the connective tissue of the spinal cord, which could lead to leakage of spinal fluid. I was always scanning my body for evidence of new numbness or weakness in one or both legs. Surely, any martial arts activity, especially the complex muscle coordination and mental attention needed to perform such feats was a distant memory. Even inching toward the physical dynamics needed to wield a sword was unfeasible. I was grounded.

My wife took care of me. My constrained daily routine involved ample bed rest with limited essential walking. I would shift from chair to chair in the house, as I could not stay comfortable in any one place for very long. I would nap on the couch. My favorite spot was on the deck in a rocking chair when the weather was nice. I could read if my mind was clear enough, but mostly I sat still as I quietly drifted through what some would call daydreaming. For me, it was more like creative journeys filled with musings and insights, pulling from memories, echoes, images, feelings, and connections to other places both of and beyond this world.

I needed this diversion because the pain remained daunting. I came out of surgery changed. I had my moments of frustration because of the discomfort and limitations imposed by the pain, yet my Zen training was a default mode that served me well by bringing me back into the imperfect yet redeemable moment. By following the rhythm of my breath, I was pulled away from my discerning mind that was interpreting the active nerve signals from my throbbing back. I knew that getting angry and defiant would only feed an unsupportive rut of resistance. I couldn't get depressed. I couldn't wallow. I needed to use my compacted strength wisely.

I was impatient. The long road to recovery was not only a nuisance, but torment for someone like me who was used to being active. The only movement the doctors sanctioned was walking. After all, even Hippocrates said, "Walking is the best medicine." But walking made the pain worse because my gait was lopsided. I was constantly off balance, holding a persistent fear that I would fall.

Several months after the surgery, I was walking in the woods alongside my property. It was a mild day in December. A branch had fallen across a fence during a storm. I wanted to see what happened. By this time, I had learned to move better—compensating and adjusting to the limitations—but I needed a cane for assistance. Walking was a chore. Both of my legs were wobbly, but I would only acknowledge that my left side was problematic. When I stepped off the path toward the fence onto some uneven ground covered with leaves, my "good leg" gave out. I fell. I didn't injure myself, but I couldn't get up.

Fortunately, I was in no danger, but as I lay there on the ground, stunned, I became livid. I crawled to a nearby tree and used mostly my upper body strength to pull myself to standing. Still furious, I realized this was only one of many annoying falls I'd endured post-surgery. My frustration, which I had kept a lid on for a long time, had reached a tipping point. Now I was seething. It was probably the first time I allowed myself to really feel my grief. The emotional pain was brutal. I was suffering. Most everything I had enjoyed and excelled at had been taken away—I could no longer walk, run, or hike. Perhaps the most disappointing and upsetting loss was an active involvement with martial arts. I could no longer spar with the sword.

Recovery is a lonely process not only because of many inconvenient limitations that upend known routines, but also because on that solitary path, it's so easy to slide into an unbalanced head space. I spent a lot of time blaming myself for what had happened, replaying the twists and turns of events, overthinking decisions I made and any discarded options. Somehow this was all my fault. Depression loomed. I was faced with periods of despair I had never experienced before.

Usually, I embrace change, as I'm open to growth and new approaches. This was different. This change was not limited to a problem-solving model where I could fix it and move on. I knew I couldn't approach this predicament with an attitude of "just work harder and eventually everything will get back to normal." Indeed, this was a clenching setback with teeth. My norms were outmoded, trampled by an unwelcome new normal. This change was more of an existential adjustment, a transformation fraught with deep emotional pain shrouded in loss. And rage.

I knew seething was unhelpful and unhealthy. I had a choice. Be miserable and devolve or focus on loving and accepting the part of me that was injured and evolve. I had to relearn how to be in my body, how to work with it rather than buttress against the barriers of my limitations. I had to release myself from blame and use pain as my guide. I had to adopt a new mode with simple instructions for myself: If it hurts, don't do it. For most folks, that makes sense. But I was used to ignoring pain and working through it. I knew the source of my discomfort was nerve pain, which is very different from the throbbing or sting of soft tissue damage.

Initially, I thought I had to learn a new way of coping. Absolutely not. I didn't need some touchy-feely, innovative technique for self-soothing. I just had to raise the bar of how I'd already managed crises throughout my entire life as a mystic—through inner alchemy and the journey within. I longed for and missed the sword. I still held in my body the ritual and dynamics of swordplay. They were ingrained in my being from lifelong training. I could seamlessly go there, on demand. The experience—detached from my body—was substantial and authentic. It was both dreamy and tangible in the Realms:

> *I feel the ground beneath my feet, I connect to the Earth with a firm stance while elongating my spine to the heavens above. I see and feel the essence and sounds of my opponent and the setting around us. I actively discern and allow as my body steps, dodges, strikes, recoils, slices, contracts, pushes, pulls. The interplay of internal and external feedback informs me while I innately respond to a dialogue of muscular engagement and mental strategy. Energy swirls like a whirlpool below and a vortex above until I transcend the here and now to connect with the One.*
>
> *Then the weapon and I disappear—from Sword to No Sword. My etheric body serves as the carriage—and then dissolves for an instant or more—surrendering to the ineffable. In that receptive place, I welcome any insight that can help me sort out my life complexities so I can move forward. I trust the Universe to help take care of me.*

One of my default modes for getting answers or advice is by accessing non-ordinary reality. I sit quietly and wait. Sometimes I see a snapshot of a person, a flash image, or a tableau. These visual sensations inform me and even inspire me to take action because they are not flat impressions. They are multidimensional. There is a clairvoyant essence to them. I've done this my whole life.

My earliest recollection of this burst of focused attention was when I was a child, perhaps eight years old. I was outside the house, playing in the yard. My mother asked me what I was doing. Without wavering and with firm confidence I replied, "I'm talking to trees." This sixth sense of connecting to the far-reaching energies beyond me has served me well throughout my entire life. More than ever, I needed guidance to help me through my challenging recovery.

It was through shamanic visions that I found or confirmed my remarkable team of healing practitioners: Kirstin for Pilates; Carol for yoga; Kevin for physical therapy; Christine for acupuncture; and Jessica, Ginnie, and Becky for energic and spiritual healing.

Kirstin instructed me on how to be agile, light, lithe, and elongated in what we comically called elfin Pilates. I learned to move through the movement more like a dancer than a boxer. That was a challenge for my football lineman body. Then Carol adapted yoga asanas for my larger frame. We named it jumbo yoga, so called because the mats were too short and narrow for me and the other equipment was much smaller than needed.

Kevin had experience training pro athletes, so he was excited to innovate rehab methods to meet my warrior-like interests. This included resistance training using kettlebells and other exercises using the Bulgarian sandbag, maces, ropes, and other Persian and Indian medieval martial training techniques.

Christine's gift surpassed classic acupuncture and herbs because she applied it all in the most loving, nurturing way. Each session felt like she was channeling the gentle touch of the goddess of compassion, Kuan Yin. Ginny and Becky worked together in the Realms on my spiritual body—the energetic resonance of my physical body. They journeyed with me to connect with the One through healing spirits and energies.

Jessica was my "no touch" Alexander practitioner and energy healer. She worked on my posture and trained me to move with maximum musculoskeletal efficiency. Uniquely, she was able to assess the misalignments in my body by tapping into its energetic frequencies. She was gifted with the ability to shift the flow of chi in my neuropathways so my body could repair and restore itself. She was the first one who was able to alleviate the pain. The effects were short-lasting because a disordered body needs to be frequently reoriented until the underlying cause is resolved.

Jessica suggested I try homeopathy, a therapeutic system that enhances one's capacity to heal by using natural substances to induce a healing response. To my surprise, my body did not respond to the homeopathic approach. Jessica balked at this. She could sense something was amiss—not with the treatment itself, but with my willingness to receive, which she called resistance.

Since I was doing everything possible to rehabilitate my body, I was stupefied to consider that maybe I was holding myself back from healing. As a psychologist, I'd seen this pattern with many of my patients. All of us develop ways of coping with the world in response and reaction to our environment. These patterns are forged throughout our childhood, a time when we are the most vulnerable. As such, we construct beliefs—many of them defenses—to keep ourselves safe and functioning as we navigate our lives. They serve an important purpose as cushions against the trials and tribulations encountered in our early years. However, when we carry forward modes that have expired, such as ways for dealing with the playground bully, a critical parent, or an overbearing boss, we end up nurturing emotional baggage. Do we ever reconsider how these ways no longer serve us?

I knew the warrior part of me held strong energies that had served me well. But had I conflated being strong-willed—my persistence and determination—with being stubborn and inflexible? Perhaps. I, too, was a creature of habit. I did what worked. I liked to think I was adaptable and open to reviewing my approach to the world. Nevertheless, when faced with this crisis—and constant pain—I found I'd shouldered the burden mostly through the lens of a warrior. It was my default mode. It's what I knew. For the warrior, vulnerability was not an option, because that would render me defenseless.

Earlier in my career as a shamanic practitioner, I discovered Ho'oponopono as a way to cultivate loving energy. I had to remind myself that Ho'oponopono was the path of the peaceful warrior. This method transmutes resistance. It nurtures surrender and acceptance. It is my go-to method with all of my patients. It works. It's simple. It changes lives. With it, I didn't have to give up my warrior roots and traits. *Surrender* is a verb, an action where I could allow my heart to open. By letting the energy flow, I could begin to love myself just as I am—warrior and all.

Jessica was right: resistance was my challenge. As I looked inside myself, I could clearly see the part of me that did not want to let the homeopathic remedy in. I began to work specifically with that part. It was the warrior who was always on guard, defending against anything looking for an inroad, which ironically, included medicine that could help.

As with most stories about healing, my path was not a straight line. Rather, there were twists and turns, stops and starts as I held resolutely to resuming my career, fostering my family connections, and enjoying my hobbies and interests. In my Framingham office, the stairs were the perfect metaphor for my mobility challenges— narrow treads with risers too high for my ability. My life was tapering like the steps. Tripping on bathroom tiles. Falling on hotel staircases. Wheelchairs in the airport. Chairlift for the office. Mobility scooter. Tractor-like machine for forest strolls. Forearm crutches. Elevator in the house to get me up to the bedroom.

Aside from the physical mobility issues, had my ego been getting in the way, tripping me up all along? Had I forgotten about the simplicity I strived for as a practitioner of Zen and overcomplicated my journey? Perhaps. But isn't that the human condition—to strive, to push back with determination when life deals you a challenging hand to play, to make lemonade from lemons?

The hardest pill to swallow was my resistance to my own evolution, but I began to see I was obstructing my own transformation. With my patients, I saw their obstinance when they entered the room—even before they sat down. Perhaps I was oblivious of my own single-minded tenacity? After all, musicians make music, teachers teach, and warriors soldier on. My patient, Rachael, reminded me of my own resistance. Rachael was frustrated and debilitated by chronic vertigo. She came to me, looking for comfort and advice.

I said, "Be brave, be gentle. Expect nothing. There is nowhere else to go but inward. I have found if you can let go of all those external strengths that define you, there is a whole new world that opens up. You just have to let it. The world will use all of what you used to be able to do, but in a totally different way that is way more powerful and useful than before. Just let it unfold by itself."

Rachael was unsure of what I meant. As a deep thinker and professional writer who was troubled by her limitations and unsure of her place in the world, she asked: "By 'let go' do you mean actually not try to think, read, write as I have? Or just to not see those things as defining me? Just keep meditating and see what comes? I know perhaps I'm being too literal here, but I do like clarity."

Rachael paused for a minute. She continued, "Hmm, maybe that's what I don't need to keep wanting. I think of the way your Power with the sword changed and increased after your surgery and loss of movement. But I don't know how you did it or how that might apply to my strengths."

I replied, "I do not know what will happen for you, but I am not talking about *not* using the gifts that define you. I am saying you will have to change how you define 'you.' Use your gifts when you can. But realize they are not you anymore. You are now something else, both more than before and different. Like me with the sword, you will have to change how you use your 'sword.' I did it by realizing what is and accepting it. I can no longer use the sword like I did."

"I realized that no matter what I did, in whatever Realm I did it in, it was not going to work if I kept expecting it to be the same as it used to be. The pain just got worse and worse. After a long while, I realized this as being 'what is.' When you get to this place of accepting what is, you change. You surrender. You let go of part of your old ego. The part that would not let go."

Rachael listened attentively. She then asked me, "What do you mean by 'surrender?'"

"Surrender," I said, "is a verb in this case. It is action. Surrender in meditation. Let your heart open. Be brave. Let the energy flow in, actively. Love you as you are. Stop fighting and resisting the change that has occurred and is happening in your life."

I continued. "Then something new happens. You become accepting of this new you. New powers will develop. Many new ways of being *you* will appear. These new ways will make use of the old you, but many other things will be added to the mix. So, ride the wave of the new you. It is exciting, beautiful, scary, and loving. Enjoy it. I have found it is much more rewarding than resisting it."

My words to Rachael resonated for me, too. How so? I approached the threshold. I challenged the guardian—the warrior in me. In mythology, the Hero's Journey is a template for the story of the hero who goes on an adventure, is victorious in a decisive crisis, and comes home changed or transformed. In the Hero's Journey, the threshold guardian is the one who holds the hero back from stepping into a new Realm, keeping them from a new way of being involved and engaged in an unfamiliar place. This was me. This was my current journey. The warrior in me was my threshold guardian. With this new awareness, I allowed myself to unfold. The butterfly released from the chrysalis. Renewal awaited me.

Or so I thought.

In March of 2020, the then-mysterious Covid-19 virus shuttered the world. Society was stunned and debilitated. Humanity—now amid a global pandemic—was consumed with fear. I stopped seeing patients at my office. Zoom video conferencing became the safe, no-contact way of interacting. My patients were struggling, mostly anxious and worried. The uncertainty caused emotional distress for many. Much of the workforce abandoned their office environments and home was no longer a place solely for respite. For some, it became a cage. Sessions with my patients were more frequent, weightier, and sadder than usual because in-person social networks and community interactions were suspended. People had more time to wrestle the thoughts swirling in their heads with fewer ways to recharge and limited options for distractions.

I was working every day of the week. The intensity weighed on me. Prior to Covid, I handled less than one-third of my caseload via telephone. Now, I was seeing everyone remotely either over the telephone or through Facetime or Zoom. The benefit of not

KOAN 4: THRESHHOLD GUARDIAN

sitting face to face with my clients was that I could laser-focus on the energetics of the situation to discern the issues and work mostly through the Realms.

The emergence of Covid shifted the dynamics of my sword class, too. For years, up to a dozen folks gathered for instruction with me for beginner-to-intermediate practice sessions that included sparring and ample social time. Since group assembly was either banned or discouraged, we could no longer meet in person. Fortunately, two of my dedicated, advanced students—Mike and John—were determined to persist because swordplay is feasible and enjoyable outside. The open air would most likely keep us from transmitting the virus if any of us carried it. My students were open to learning more about how I used the sword for connecting with the One.

Together, we created a learning lab with no agenda or lesson plans, using a variety of weapons—European, Chinese, and Japanese long and short swords; spears; and the *jo*, a Japanese wooden staff.

This format was ideal for us to use my Radical Freedom technique, allowing each person to find their own way of connecting to the One, because nothing is prescribed. We were more than just a martial arts practice pod. We became family through an energetic bond. We shared our life stories and challenges, all the while sharpening our martial skills with our synergy. This intention reminded me of the old Zen saying: the student must equal or best their teacher or both have failed. Together, we honed the Sword of No Sword concept, of slipping through the time-space continuum. I made several spirit contacts including with Ueshiba, the father of Aikido. It was both thrilling and satisfying. To date, we still meet each Saturday to train.

In April of 2021, a year after the emergence of Covid, the fabric of society was still entangled with fear and uncertainty. Fear penetrated deeper into my personal world as well. I was diagnosed with prostate cancer. Cancer is frightening because it is mostly seen as a vicious, unpredictable enemy. Moreover, the treatment process is usually painful, and its aftereffects significantly reduce the quality of life. On my Hero's Journey, cancer was an additional rut on the road of trials, yet another boogeyman lurking from the shadows to unnerve me. The warrior in me was already tired. He was now called to action with a renewed determination to overcome an unforeseen—and potentially deadly—adversary.

I'd been in this place before with my spinal column narrative. I researched the best doctors in Boston. A whirlwind of medical diagnostics and discussions about interventions snowballed. Biopsies, MRIs, ultrasounds, and other imaging. Consultations. Blood test after blood test. Weighing options. Investigating cause and effect. Eventually, I surrendered to a conventional allopathic intervention that included one year of drug and radiation treatment.

To face this challenge, I doubled down on what worked in the past—focus and discipline—to keep from getting overwhelmed and to steer toward the best outcome. That meant I was living an inverted life, as in downward dog, the yoga pose where the body assumes an inverted V shape with the hands and feet on the floor, blood rushing to the head, and the buttocks pointing upward. No matter how unpleasant or uncomfortable the path was for fighting cancer, I had to keep to my empowering daily practices, especially meditation and connecting through the Realms with the One.

For the first time in my life, I had to stop seeing patients. My life came to a screeching halt. The aftereffects of the treatment affected my ability to focus, my stamina, and my head space. I was exhausted and, in some ways, ineffectual. My body and mind were compromised. I was faced with a quandary where I felt adrift from the identity I had crafted throughout a lifetime. It was like looking at a once-completed puzzle, but now, all the pieces were scattered, exposing missing sections.

Each day, I asked myself, *Who am I today? What's important?* I barely had the strength to ask or envision *What's next?* I recalled, from my trip to Córdoba many years ago, the words of Seneca: "Pray for a sound mind and good health, first of soul and then of body." Seneca, as a disciple of Socrates (although living a half millennium beyond him) had echoed crucial words from his teacher—soul first, then body. I understood the mission: I had to emphasize my inner resources to overcome the physical limitations that had undermined my quality of life. Socrates taught that we are not to be identified with what we own, our social status, our reputation, or even our body. Instead, Socrates famously maintained that our true self is our soul. Our body is just the vehicle.

I have become anchored in the mundane, I thought, *a worn body*. My body had endured a boxing match, taking punches. When knocked down, it flinched, endured the pain, and eventually found a way of getting back up, even if that meant I was disoriented and staggering to my feet. But I couldn't dismiss a stark reality: my strength had diminished. I knew this with heart-rending certainty. Within me, the determined warrior was ready to don his armor and fight to the end, like a scrappy brawler, no matter how compromised he may be.

"Now what?" I ask myself in a shamanic-like trance.

I can sense the warrior part of me is terrified.

"Are you afraid of dying?" I ask.

"No," comes the answer. "You know that is not how a warrior acts. I am afraid of being pushed to the side and forgotten about. I do not want to be irrelevant. I do not want to be invisible."

I try to reassure him. "What we are doing is transmuting our energy. We have to change. The old ways are not working. We have gotten too old. Before we run out of time, we need to become something else. Remember the bodhisattva vows. In order to get there, we cannot go on like we have been. Look where it has gotten us. If we keep going on like this there will be nothing left of our body to do or help anyone."

This seems to help some, but I can tell we are not there yet.

"We need to get this done," I say. "I am tired of playing this game. You get most of my attention all the time. We need to change this because I am moving on. Are you coming with me?"

I realize, even though I am still having trouble with this metamorphosis, lots has changed. I am getting tired of having to recover from these physical life emergencies. My being knows of my vow when I was twenty to make an offering of my life. In this lifetime, that is my purpose. However, I find that my karma is very heavy to bear. It is like carrying a heavy load of armor. Armor from many past lifetimes of being a warrior, both good and bad. I felt a clear, energetic reverberation. If I take a little of the armor off, then everything else in my being collapses.

I knew I was the Red Dragon, that persona I cultivated through years of Zen studies and countless hours of meditation. He was a mystic who transcended the mundane. He knew the warrior had been pushed to the far edge of the threshold and needed to step through the doorway. That was where the Power was—through inner alchemy and the journey within, I could free myself of my mind chatter, my stories, my emotional baggage. Then I could connect to the One with clarity. That's where the actual Power was.

I've lived this. My patients remind me almost daily that we all have defensive mechanisms we use to protect ourselves. They were effective tools when we most needed them, usually in childhood. But carried forward, they become a hindrance. For my patients, I hold space for them to explore the stories they carry about their life journeys. My role is to facilitate their exploration of new ways, new Powers, novel and forgotten ways of being and doing.

My warrior self was being called to that ineffable place beyond the threshold, that symbolic gateway in the Hero's Journey where resurrection and rebirth present a road back. In some traditions, this was known as returning with the elixir. The restorative medicine, per se, was not a tincture or a pill. It was a discovery. That finding led to an encounter. That encounter flowered into a profound spiritual experience replete with a path to self-reconciliation.

Recovery was slow and frustrating. I slept a lot. One day when reviewing emails on my computer, I saw a book recommendation from Amazon. It was *Be Love Now* by Ram Dass. I had not read any of his works in many years. At first, I thought the title was a mistake, as I was remembering one of his most famous books, *Be Here Now*, published in 1972. I recalled reading and liking that book because the premise promoted Zen elements—be present, stay in the moment, focus. The full title of the newer book especially intrigued me. *Be Love Now: The Path of the Heart.*

Perhaps this is a timely reminder, I wondered, *a message from the Universe?* It echoed how I used Ho'oponopono daily to transmute frustration, pain, and anger. Love as the foundation for healing is potent.

When I was in middle school, I read about Israel ben Eliezer, known as the Baal Shem Tov (Speaker of the Good Names). He was a Jewish mystic and healer regarded as the founder of the modern Hassidic movement from the Russian Pale of Settlement of the early to mid-1700s. He believed in direct connection with the divine with no middleman, per se, to make that happen. The Jewish mystics believed Hebrew letters and numbers contained supernatural or spiritual energy. Also, prayer was of supreme importance, although I suspect that prayer was a form of meditation because worshippers were encouraged to follow their distracting thoughts until finding their roots nestled in the divine.

This is like Zen practice. These rabbis helped people overcome problems so they could heal by using mindfulness practice while guiding them to connecting with God—the One. Wasn't this the primary shamanic technique I used with all my patients? I found it fascinating that, at the time, the Baal Shem Tov did not insist on the study of scriptures to connect to God. Rather, attention and focus with loving intention was the key. As a preteen, the simplicity had appealed to me: Love God with mind and heart. That's straightforward. No middleman. Just do it.

This uncomplicated approach of the Baal Shem Tov reminded me of a similar practice used by the Japanese monk Nichiren, the founder of Pure Land Buddhism started in the 1300s. In this school, there was an essential method for connecting to the

One: chanting a mantra. This persistent focus was key to releasing emotional and mental gridlock. There's no doubt that an unwavering echo of a mantra repeated all day would eventually help one let go of all other thoughts encumbering the mind. Again, this technique was straightforward, with no middleman. If you want results, then just do it.

When *Be Here Now* was first published, it was very exciting for Americans who were seeking solace to hear stories of an Indian guru imparting wisdom. I was also fascinated by the tales Ram Dass told of his teacher, Neem Karoli Baba. I was in my late teens, at a crossroads, and seeking life direction. I chose between studying Zen or becoming a disciple of Ram Dass. The guru track seemed convoluted to me. Even then, I was cagey, careful not to commit to a fixed, singular path. I needed options without the pressure of manmade, external obligations with all the ceremony and fanfare. Zen felt unassuming and less problematic. I wasn't looking for an easy path, just one that was direct, without embellishments. Zen made sense to me—empty your mind, let go of your ego, wait for grace to connect to the One.

I also felt that Ram Dass sounded like a classic Harvard lecturer, persistently talking about his guru, Baba, which is the honorific Hindu word for "father," "grandfather," "wise old man," "guru," or "sir." That's one reason why I lost interest. I just was never captivated by the whole guru thing, mostly because, as I realized later, it's not Radical Freedom. I was suspicious of giving it all up to another person; that is, dedicating focus, time, and attention to someone who is believed to have the answers. It felt culty to me. The lack of personal agency in that model really concerned me fifty years ago, and that feeling has stayed with me.

Be Here Now doesn't necessarily claim that having a guru is the way out. But it does make clear that the guru is an important, tethered resource. Overall, the stories piece together a theme that asks us what we are willing to do for love and happiness and to consider how we create meaning in our lives. Remembering this book while going through my cancer recovery was yet another timely reminder and message from the Universe. I immediately thought of the scattered pieces of my own existential puzzle. Deepening the love could be one path for healing for myself. Just the concept of be love now vibrated for me. I had to know more.

One night in early August of 2022, I was restless after dinner. I did not want to read, so I searched through streaming video services for documentaries. I came across one that told of a yogi's experience. It followed the typical suburban enlightenment story: In the sixties, a young guy drops out of school, does drugs, goes to India, meets his guru Ram Dass, becomes a disciple, leaves India, goes back to school, resumes his suburban life. I was underwhelmed. I wanted to turn it off because I was fidgety. But each time a video clip of Ram Dass's guru, Baba, came on, it gave me pause. There was something about him that captivated me. When Baba appeared on the screen, his eyes were speaking explicitly to me. I felt an incomprehensible powerful resonance. He spoke directly to my soul.

The documentary continued. The suburban yogi returned to India in search of what he did not find all those years ago, a classic story of reclamation. In his pilgrimage, he visited some of Baba's *ashrams*, schools the guru either founded or oversaw. Since Baba had died decades prior in 1973, the yogi interviewed the current head priests. In one exchange, the yogi expressed disappointment that he never got to meet Baba. In response, the cleric somewhat chides the yogi: "It does not matter. He is always here for you. All you have to do is to call on him."

Immediately, I relax.
I call on Baba.
I expand my consciousness outward, losing track of time and space.
I feel myself enter the Realms.
I sense a portal or doorway of sorts where I step off and then jump in, ignoring any resistance.
I am both freefalling and embracing at the same time.
I allow. I am open.
I trust that I've landed in the right place.
Indeed, the right place is in Baba's light and love.

Later on, I chided myself: *Why didn't I think of just connecting with him before?* I had called on lots of souls for help and guidance. Most times when I called, they came. The experience of connecting to Baba was similar to how I connected with any other ancestor, energy, or soul. But why now? Why had I become drawn to Baba and his grace?

From a practical perspective, healing is a process. It may take years of revisiting our problems, peeling back and exposing the layers to unmask energetic build-up and any karmic residue in preparation for liberating our travails. Often, psychospiritual and emotional healing happens in an instant—a sacrosanct, notable moment when we accept a shift in consciousness, an integration of our pain, sorrow, and anguish. It is a tipping point. Our story changes from one of struggle and suffering to self-surrender and acceptance. In many ways, we call a truce, a ceasefire within ourselves to allow for a peace agreement. This is a remarkable transformation, a positive change that impacts our lives going forward. It affects the choices we make from that moment and beyond on how we navigate our world. It is potent and empowering because we can't go back. We've moved on, from stuck to unstuck.

Meeting Baba—a remote yet intimate encounter—was a transcendent experience. I was open. I let him in. I allowed him to bless me with his wisdom and guidance. As a mystic, I seek out contemplation and must continually self-surrender to find unity with the One. Baba stirred within me a curiosity to both listen to my disquiet and look deeper at the shadows. But first, he left a trail of symbolic crumbs for me to follow—from what seemed like a mysterious email about a book that led me to a video documentary centered around the framework of his student Ram Dass. I revisited an old story with a new twist.

This new contact with Baba was the elixir—the healing remedy—from my Hero's Journey for confronting the threshold guardian, the warrior in me. After my first encounter with Baba, I was compelled to return to deepen my connection:

It is total light, total love.

A brilliant golden light, so bright, even with my eyes closed, they clench, like staring into the sun.

This is not akin to love from the heart.

It is so much more.

It is an all-encompassing, expansive, ineffable yet nurturing, relatable love from connecting to the One.

For the ensuing months to come, I connected to Baba daily, seeking his wisdom and allowing him to carry me even deeper into an experience of the One. Almost like a science fiction mission, I found a wormhole to another dimension. It was a quantum leap of consciousness. Baba brought me to a place where self-reconciliation could unfurl:

> *Basking.*
>> *Total light, total love.*
>> *The light still blinding.*
>> *My heart so full.*
>> *Expansive. Ineffable. Nourishing.*
>> *No body. No time. No place. No thought.*
>> *No process. No intention.*
>> *Nothing.*
>> *And everything.*
>> *It just is.*
>> *The true beauty of the experience is Zen.*
>> *Being.*
>> *The moment is salient and simple.*
>> *All of life's complications are stripped away.*
>> *My tightly wound warrior energy dissipates.*

This was a lot like being in dokusan when I was in the Zendo over forty years before. It was an assessment, of sorts, where the teacher and student sit face to face, the Roshi looking for confirmation of a mind-to-mind transmission. Pressure built with each brief encounter over a period of years until I finally released the encumbrances of my mind constructs, those which anchored me from welcoming catharsis and clarity. Once I let go, the koan—the riddle—was solved.

And what of the warrior? He had gone nowhere. He was still part of me. My quest was to further integrate his energy and his Power, not to exile him. He had served me well for my entire life.

My connection to him was long overdue for a re-evaluation, as he was typecast as the protective, defensive protagonist who, always watchful and often suspicious, would stand down until needed. He had been confused, since cancer struck, as to his role. The decline in my energy—my vital life force—rendered him weakened and unsure of how he could serve me in a re-visioned life. I no longer needed to be the hawk, on the hunt, searching for prey. The warrior became more of a guide. The warrior willingly renounced his role as the threshold guardian for the Hero's Journey to conclude. I entered the Realms:

With the Warrior soothed, what now?

He has not been neutralized. He has not been neutered. He remains strong. What do I—John, the aging man in his early seventies with a compromised body—have to lose? My anger. My frustrations. My wrangling with the banal, especially the scuffle with physical pain and my attachment to the life I crafted and hoped to restore. Only through Baba did I see I was mired in a muddle of routine anguish that anchored me to emotional and spiritual suffering.

What do I have to gain? Freedom. In that place of love and grace held by Baba, I am unscathed.

I really had no option if I truly wanted reconciliation. I had to surrender to the One. This I already knew, as I had been investing so much effort toward finding an answer. I was sure resolution could be found by connecting to the One. Baba showing me the way was an unexpected gift. I had to let go of my guru bias, as that story no longer served me. The warrior would be integrated by and through love. Unquestionably, love changed the energetic narrative and approach—which I was keenly aware of and used with my patients.

KOAN 4: THRESHHOLD GUARDIAN

Then there was a moment, like a parachuter at the door of the airplane, when the expanse called. Baba was my guide:

This time I am called by love. Such love. Amplified. Resounding. Vibrating. Baba takes me through a gateway/vortex. Vastness. Transcendence. The One. Surpassing all prior encounters. Beyond words. There is great Power here. Baba fades, dissolves. I return. Yet I remain.

Months later, Baba was still with me. I called on him every day. I studied his teachings and discovered they were quite simple, akin to Nichiren and the Baal Shem Tov, with their streamlined connections to the One. This was the best Way for me. It might be the *only* Way for me. I learned that Baba practiced Bhakti yoga, the yoga of love and service. There is no dogma, just love through the cultivation and expression of loving intentions. Ram Dass was right: the path of the heart is to *be love now*. Embracing love is quite different than being love. It took me many years to allow such beauty to surround me and then permeate my essence. There was great Power in that state of being.

Now that the warrior and I were reconciled, he guided me to Baba with each journey to the Realms. He would also become instrumental with forthcoming shamanic workings, helping me lead souls in distress to the light.

I realized I had solved my first life koan. I had transmuted my warrior energy into healing energy. This transformation served me in solving my next life koan when I was subsequently called to release trapped souls. These souls had haunted me for my entire life by echoing in the Realms.

QUESTIONS FOR SELF-REFLECTION

- What holds you back?

- What is keeping you from getting to where you want to be?

- What's in the way?

- What are your defense mechanisms?

- How can you challenge and release your *threshold guardian*?

- What is the Power beyond your fear and limitations?

KOAN 5

Driving to the hospital.

Something is off. A horrible feeling. Getting more intense the closer I get.

Fear. Heavy air, reeking of sweat. Intense crying. Wailing. I'm not alone. Many others. Dread. Alarm.

We are sheep being rounded up—for slaughter.

The hospital buildings look like the camp itself. Low brick buildings spread out. I was there. In the camp. Not a daydream or trick of the mind. An energetic flashback.

Death. And more death. Panic. Why did I allow this? Why did I not fight?

Jolting back to the present. Indoors, now. The waiting area for radiation treatment. Unnerved. In a cold, anxious sweat.

I've always held this fear. The terror of the camp sits in my third chakra, the place of personal Power. It affects everything I do.

Echoes in the Realms

My earliest memories—perhaps when I was two or three years old—are of my previous past life where I was killed in a Nazi concentration camp. I was too young to know what I was experiencing, so I just buried it. Every now and again, the terrible images would resurface. What could I do? I was a kid. I felt the fear, smelled death and the gas. I saw each brick on the buildings. It was very real to me. It was horrifying. My parents thought I was just having nightmares and figured I would just outgrow it. The flashbacks continued, so I just stopped telling them how they lingered. My parent's generation grew up with the Holocaust. As a Jew, this wasn't some illusive historical event. The war ended just six years prior to my birth in 1952. My family—and all Jews—lived with this pall of terror.

In my early teens, I came across a book that confirmed I wasn't crazy: *From Ashes to Healing: Mystical Encounters with the Holocaust* by Yonassan Gershom. I was relieved to know other people had similar stories to tell.

One day, in the early 2000s, I was meeting with a patient in my office, Gwen. We had worked together for many years. I respected her abilities. She had a high IQ and was a seer with the gift for looking both forward and backward in time. We were working through a concern when Gwen stopped mid-sentence. She asked, "Do you smell gas?"

It was winter and the heat was on. Since my office building was built somewhere around 1900, I immediately thought there was a leak. Right then, I was struck by a very powerful smell. I knew it well. It was not from the radiator in the building. It was the smell of the gas chambers—a pungent, acrid odor, mixed with the stench of burning flesh.

Just then, we were both drawn into a huge energy surge. It enveloped the room. It induced a trance state.

I glanced at Gwen. I could see she was there, too, both of us in the Realms. Her torso started to sway. Her hand carved circular patterns in the air, distinctive movements she made when she received psychic visions. I, on the other hand, got quite still when I connected to the Realms.

"Oh my!" she said. "I think we are in a concentration camp. These memories are not yours."

I was speechless. And startled.

"This is the Holocaust," Gwen noted. "These experiences are not yours. They belong to someone else," she said with absolute certainty.

I look around. Yes, I am back in the concentration camp. I'm not sure if it is the same as the one I saw in my childhood, but it is a camp, nonetheless.

This time, however, I see and feel something beyond the terror. It is something amazing and transformative.

When Gwen speaks, I sense a being, or perhaps it is an energy field, moving away from me.

I see a flash of light, bright and golden.

> *Then everything turns golden, and I feel an enormous wave of compassion embrace me. I don't resist. I let it happen. All the darkness I always had around me when I was in the camp lifted.*
>
> *Is it the bodhisattva of compassion, Kuan Yin? Has she just blessed me with her presence? I know of her energy from prior experiences. It is always a golden light, warm, loving, and compassionate. It takes my breath away.*
>
> *This encounter is unique, though. It is deeper, more profound. Maybe she is a messenger from the One? I think it is Grace—the word of God.*
>
> *Then the whole presence moves away into the light.*
>
> *I am completely overcome.*
>
> *Also a Rebbe, a Hassidic orthodox Jewish spiritual leader, looks up and smiles at me. He is in a temple with many long tables where rabbis are praying and studying.*

Time stopped. All of this unfolded between Gwen's words. She was not aware of what was happening to me. She was entranced. I was no longer in my body. I was immersed in a quantum leap into another reality. This was very real. I was there—wherever "there" was. Although I was somewhere else, I was held in the awesome presence and Power of the One.

Gwen wasn't the first to tell me these experiences were not mine despite how I was immersed in them. Two other psychics confirmed this. Each time the psychics repeated their message, I could not verify their statements. Yes, I clearly heard what they said—"These experiences are not yours." Even though I understood the words they spoke, when I looked in the Realms, I couldn't see anything of concern. I was confused. If I can't see something, then words alone don't have the ability or Power to shift my experience. I can't make sense of it. It's empty. When I work shamanically, if I don't see it, it's just not real to me.

In the days that followed, the essence of that warm compassion remained. Indeed, I was blessed with Kuan Yin's love and her compassion for me. Also, I realized that Grace was there to help me but in some unknown way I was yet to discover. The experience was so beautiful. When it was over, I was sure it had to be a bodhisattva—a spiritual teacher—who came to impart some significant understanding or wisdom.

I puzzled over what I was to learn. I thought: *How should I interpret this transformation?* Also, I was perplexed. *Did I really have a past life in the Holocaust? Was that truly a bodhisattva experience? Whoever's memory it was (how could it not be mine?), why would I need to experience the Holocaust at all?* Maybe I was like Milarepa, one of Tibet's most famous yogis and spiritual poets. Often, his story is used as an allegorical teaching about humility.

Milarepa's teacher, Marpa, could see his student was powerful yet arrogant. Milarepa was given the task of hauling rocks to the top of a hill to build a stone house. When completed, he was quite pleased with himself. Marpa then told him, "Very nice, but I made a mistake, the stone house needs to be on another hill." So, Milarepa dragged the stones up another hill and built another house. Tired, but proud of having accomplished the labor, again his teacher proclaimed, "Mistake. Build it on the next hill." The trial continued until Milarepa got the message—Don't be proud and arrogant. Just do the task at hand. Stay in the moment, nothing else.

Was my experience of pain and suffering a trial to teach me not to be proud and arrogant, as I certainly had been in earlier lives as a soldier and shamanic warrior? Or maybe the dark experience was to help me feel the pain and suffering of others? Since I am exceptionally empathic, this did not make sense to me.

A few weeks later, Gwen and I met again. We weren't expecting to talk about my earlier experience, for she had another topic to address. As soon as she sat down though, we entered yet another trance state. We were back at the camp.

I see a man standing in front of me. He wears the striped uniform of the camp.

He approaches me and says, "Thank God you have come. I have been waiting for you for a very long time."

He is quite thin and emaciated with big blue eyes. Despite the horrors around him, he seems to have no fear. He is very loving and exudes compassion. He feels like some sort of Tzadik, a good, wise man and Rabbi or guru rolled into one.

He continues: "I know I'm going to die soon. I am not afraid. I want to pass on a gift to you, as it had been given to me."

Then, he gifts me love and compassion.

His lips don't move, but I hear his voice inside my head saying, "This is a very ancient gift that has been handed down to me."

He reaches out through time and empowers me in the same way buddhas and bodhisattvas pass on dharma transmission. The gift is not a thing, it's an experience that opens me. Dharma transmission is a mind-to-mind experience, an energetic exchange. The Tzadik opens up an inimitable space in time where I am able to step into for this to happen.

The experience is not rooted in any specific religion. It seems like a pure energy transfer, like being embraced by the Universe. I become one with Being, a pervasive Unity, and allow myself to experience Grace, the word of God—the One.

I let go. I allow. I don't resist. I know I have to let go of any disquiet so I can connect to something more. I know when a part of me transmuted fear then I could step through that threshold and expand my consciousness. This loosening will allow certain energy to be transmitted to me.

I then ask him, "Why did I have to undergo years of darkness and painful awareness of the camp?"

Silence.

Was this yet another koan to balance my gift of Power?

Then he replies: "Yes. This was a test. We wanted to see if you could handle the darkness and pain before passing on the gift to you."

He dissolves into light. He is gone.

A Rebbe looks up and smiles at me. He is in a temple with many long tables where rabbis are praying and studying.

I suppose, somehow, I passed the test. Why me? I have no idea. Probably, the man who brought me the gift of Grace had been with me all my life. And I wonder if he was with me during my earliest memories of the camp, as a child.

Maybe I hadn't been ready until that moment. The best I could figure is all the work I'd done through the decades—my entire life—got me to a place where I was prepared for the encounter so I would then use the insight wisely.

I've always been able to send focused energy. That is one of my skills, one of my gifts. Now I need to learn how to channel and focus this new gift, the Grace.

In my daily meditations, I worked on being in that field of Grace. Yet I knew there was more to this story. It felt unfinished.

Some twelve years later, I was with Ginnie, a strong, passionate seer. She is psychic and a dedicated healer. We were talking. She stopped mid-sentence and asked: "Do you smell gas?"

KOAN 5: ECHOES IN THE REALMS

Astonished, I thought, *Oh, here we go again.*

"Oh my! Are we in a Nazi concentration camp?" Ginnie asked. She knew nothing about my past life experiences in the camp. She seemed agitated.

Ginnie continued: "This is real. You are there, too. I see all these souls. They are waiting for you."

Still stunned, I thanked her for the unexpected reading. We continued and completed our conversation.

As she got up from the couch and started walking toward the door, she turned to me and said: "You may not believe it. But you were there with me. I saw all the souls waiting for you. You did not want to see them, but they are there—waiting for *you.*"

I thought, *I don't know what to make of this.*

The next morning in meditation I knew it was important to find out more about this situation.

I enter the Realms to return to the camp. It is the same one Gwen had seen. Now Ginnie. Ginnie saw what was happening in the camp.

Yes. Ginnie was right, there are souls waiting for me—hundreds and hundreds and hundreds of them. A sea of beings of light.

A deep voice—I think it is male, but I'm not sure—reverberates in my being.

It speaks.

"They have been waiting for you, for many years. You are to release them—release them back to the light."

Energy swirls. Then vibrations. I am in a tunnel—but not—moving through somewhere yet nowhere, surrounded by powerful, condensing energy. I know I have to surrender to it, to let go of anything that defines me. I cannot resist or try to control it, or it will dissolve. As I embrace it, a beautiful blue light appears. It is concentrated and strong. The Power continues to build.

The voice directs me.

"You are to use the blue light to release these souls back to the light."

For the next three days, I did as I was charged.

I open up a space above the souls. I use the blue light as a beacon to draw the souls toward what seems like a vortex, pulling them both above and away from me. I can sense other gentle, loving energetic beings helping me do this. It is beautiful, beyond words. I can sense joy from the souls who have been freed. When the final soul is released, the camp disappears. It is an amazing experience. Such beauty.

Again, a Rebbe looks up and smiles at me. He is in a temple with many long tables where rabbis are praying and studying.

I didn't understand this recurring vision. Why me? Why did I have to release these souls? Why were they waiting for me? What happened to the camp? Was any of this real?

A few weeks later Ginnie and I met, again. I asked her these exact questions.

She replied: "They were waiting for you because of your Power with light. You were their leader. And so you were the only one who could release them."

Her response made me more curious. Why did this happen? Exactly what is the gift? Why me? Why do I need someone else to help me see? Why did I need Ginnie, specifically, to do this?

"Leader?" I asked. "Leader of what?"

KOAN 5: ECHOES IN THE REALMS

Panic attacks. Unresolved Fear. More flashbacks. What is going on?

After my prostate cancer diagnosis in April of 2021, I carefully thought through my options with my family and medical team. I decided not to have surgery. I chose to undergo radiation as the remedy to help my body heal.

I drove myself each time for treatment, from my home in the greater Boston suburbs to the hospital, the Dana Farber/Brigham Cancer Center nestled in the Boston medical district. It is a relatively short trip, just sixteen miles, but it can take up to sixty minutes due to traffic snafus.

Within the first few weeks, I had panic attacks both before and during the treatments. They started an hour or two before I left the house. I would just panic—anxiety, cold sweats, and ominous fear wedged in my solar plexus. It felt like there was a resistant field of energy I was pushing against. As I got closer to the hospital, it would increase. *This makes no sense*, I told myself. I knew the roads and the route. Once at the hospital, I knew the treatment routine, too, yet the unease and dread would peak. This response was so out of character for me, the warrior who could regulate his emotions and push through any adversity.

I consulted with Fiona, one my trusted healer friends. She echoed both Gwen and Ginnie's visions—she saw the concentration camp. I trusted her implicitly, as she was never wrong, always spot on.

Back on the meditation cushion, I focused my attention on this recurring scenario. Undeniably, the hospital was triggering memories of the camp. But why?

I reached out to a colleague of mine, Denise, a radiation oncologist who was guiding me through the whole cancer treatment process. Her insight helped me make some sense of the flashbacks.

"I've seen this many times," she told me, "with Jewish patients."

Taken aback, I reacted, "Oh my! Why is that?"

Denise continued: "I think there's a connection to the tiny tattoo you get at the hospital. It is used as a marker to aid the technicians so they can line up the radiation machine. There's a range of folks who experience this, from actual Holocaust survivors who endured the horrors inside the concentration camps and even some people who had not been imprisoned there. I think the tattoo is an emotional trigger."

Now I get it. But still, my visions are vivid and so disturbing.

Cattle cars. Fear. Crying. Absolute terror. The brick on the hospital buildings seem familiar. To me, it is the camp.

My rational mind is overtaken. Somehow, when nearing the hospital, I get pushed into the Realms and backward in time.

I am helpless, surrounded by cruelty and death.

Each ride to the hospital is alarming. I feel like I am driving myself to my own death.

Gas chambers. Slaughter. Doom.

I balk. Why am I doing this?

Why did I not fight?

Each time I arrived and got settled in the waiting area at the hospital, I was flustered, upset, confused, and in a cold sweat. And yet all the people in the hospital—the parking attendants, receptionists, radiation technicians, doctors, and nurses—were so kind.

I had to figure out what was going on. I needed to face this head on.

In meditation, I called on that part of me—the boy or young man—who was in the concentration camp. He was incoherent with deep-seated fear and rage.

I knew that only a loving approach would help, so I embraced him as best I could. I used Ho'oponopono to transmute the host of strong emotions that were paralyzing and harming me. I needed to turn the fear and rage into healing emotions, like love and compassion.

In a relatively short time, I did create a shift. I got the past-life me in the concentration camp to calm down enough so I could get through the yearlong radiation treatment process. Yet unease and apprehension were pervasive. My body was compromised. I was far from being healthy or well. I endured until the last day of radiation, when I collapsed at home. I was exhausted and diminished. The radiation took all the yin chi from my body and the harsh prescription drugs took all the yang chi. I felt like an empty, angry shell of a person.

Nonetheless, I knew I had to rally the will to transmute the fear from the concentration camp because the story had lingered. My body was affecting my ability to mentally focus. And psychically, there was an unresolved resonance of the camp. I could still feel strong undercurrents of fear.

Determined to regain my physical strength and mental clarity, I crafted a wellness regimen. Yoga. Pranayama breath control. Qigong. Herbs. Acupuncture. I used all these techniques in the past successfully when dealing with my asthma to raise the chi of my lungs. I have always had a problem with breathing too fast, which is a common asthmatic trait. Slowing down breathing is critical for cultivating relaxation to open the lungs. My strategy was a good one, because I was healing, albeit slowly. I used a common breathing technique taught in yoga that suggests a drawn-out breath of five-and-a-half seconds in and five-and-a-half seconds out to achieve a deep, relaxed, spiritual state. I practiced this technique daily for a month, often for an hour. I got the results I expected—I calmed down.

Yet, something was in the way. It was familiar, although undefined. I have felt this "something" all my life. I was determined to figure out what was blocking my chi.

One morning, while practicing the slow breathing I entered a blissful, healing state.

> *In a flash, I am back in the concentration camp.*
>
> *I feel fear. And I can see it, too. It looks like a dark, ominous, swirling cloud, blocking my path.*
>
> *I look directly at the fear. I walk toward it. My arms are open and extended. I welcome it. I embrace it.*
>
> *In some ways, this is how I deal with fear in ordinary reality. Yang emotions must be defused and neutralized, or they become consuming. This is an essential technique I use in the Realms.*
>
> *I know I cannot back down once I make the overture. If I renege, the fear will amplify like a propagating virus.*
>
> *I embrace the fear and hold it tightly as I invoke loving energy to emanate through me.*
>
> *This is how I transmute fear. To me, it is like riding a wave. I use my breath to support the flow of the upsurge from swell to crest and then dispersion. I stay with the current for as long as I have to until the vibe transforms from negative to neutral energy. The loving energy inundates and discharges the fear.*

I repeated this method for over a year because the fear was a form of post-traumatic stress disorder (PTSD) carried over from my prior life. Whether in ordinary reality or in the Realms, clearing energy is often not a one-and-done matter. Sometimes it requires long-term practice—and lots of patience.

KOAN 5: ECHOES IN THE REALMS

A year later, I could still sense fear lodged in my solar plexus, in the third chakra. My practice was to journey into that part of me that inhabits that Power center, that place of personal strength that fuels our ability to act in the world. But the fear continued to build up until my mind froze—I was blocked. It was like pressing up against a barricade. I could touch the obstacle but not pierce it. Daily, I rode the wave to release the fear, each time believing I had made progress. But for some unknown reason, the fear would return.

I decided I needed to go back to the camp in the Realms. I would relive the time when I received the gift of Grace. I needed to reengage all my senses so I could connect with my whole body, mind, and spirit. I needed to evoke all the associated physical and mental sensations—especially of time and of place. It was like recreating a scene from a movie I had seen in the past. All the details had to be reconstructed. It took a few days, but I did it.

I reminded myself of the intention and method. I received the gift of Grace so I could release souls into the light. To do so, I had to transmute any fear and pain. Once I was in a grounded, balanced state, I could invoke the light, directing the fear and pain that was encased in any darkness toward that light.

This time, the transmutation was in service to me.

I begin to ride the wave. I scan for the fear. I can't find it. Something is different. The block is gone. The fear is absent. My third chakra glows. I feel only light and Grace enveloping me.

Then I have a flashback. I am eighteen. I feel my warrior energy. It is robust, impatient—and angry. I am inexperienced and untrained. I have youthful vitality. I am driven.

I know hard karate won't serve me. I need to learn internal martial arts, Qigong, meditation. All this will lead me down the path to Zen. Unexpectedly, shamanism will keep calling me, too.

There is a knowing. I need to focus on a path of transformation, from dark warrior to being of light. At eighteen, I don't know what that means. It is a clear message but with no clear-cut instructions. Somehow, I always get directed toward loving ways and I connect with people who guide me on my path.

The deep-rooted fear is gone. I feel great joy. And bliss. I realize the shift away from fear and toward love has been a persistent, arduous undertaking for more than fifty years. And here it is. Here I am, fear-less. Liberated. The moment is defining.

Emanating golden light surrounds me. It is gentle, yet powerful. Glowing. Softly vibrating.

And now blue. The Blue Pearl—the light that illuminates the mind, that illuminates everything. It is said to contain the entire Universe and divinity within the individual. Clear. Insightful. Powerful. It is Power I can use for myself and to help others.

The mysterious, repetitive vision returns—a Rebbe looks up and smiles at me. He is in a temple with many long tables where rabbis are praying and studying.

The bliss faded quickly. A month later, I was still so tired—bone-weary tired. Drained. I could not sleep. I was often bloated. These were common effects of radiation treatments.

Why was I not healing? Was it the fear resurfacing?

KOAN 5: ECHOES IN THE REALMS

Somehow, I was getting in my own way. And, yes—there was fear. But this fear felt instinctive and primordial. Warrior fears. The fear of dying. The fear of being who I am. The fear of not being able to recover. The fear of weakening. What if I could no longer defend myself?

The cancer treatments diminished me physically. They muddled my thinking by further compromising my body and imposing even more limits.

Now what? I had to walk my talk. I needed to embrace the fear, this existential fear. And work toward transmuting it.

Panic returned. Not related to the hospital. Not connected to the camp. I needed advice. I sought out Jessica, again.

"What's going on, John?" she asked.

"I was having panic attacks before and during treatments at the hospital."

"I still see the concentration camp," she said. "I feel the fear. I see a child. He's afraid."

I thought, *A child? Is she talking about me? I don't sense him.* I questioned her, "Are you sure that's me?"

I entered the Realms to find out more.

Unknowingly, Jessica creates a space between me and the child from the camp.

The child Jessica is connecting to is not me. The fear feels like it belongs to someone else. Did someone or something attach to me? I've felt this fear my entire life and thought it was mine. But now I don't think so. I am sure it belonged to another.

I can clearly see a soul has been attached to me all along. If the energy were mine, it would have a warrior signature. I have a knowing that most of my past lives were as a soldier or warrior. So, the little boy energy seems out of place.

The puzzle is unraveling. There are two concurrent fears at play: mine as a teenager in the camp and this young boy's, too.

For the first time, I can see the boy.

Had I picked up this soul in utero? Or maybe at the moment of my birth, he attached to me? I think I have been carrying this possession my whole life.

The situation was ironic. As a shamanic practitioner, I assessed other people's energy. From the moment they walked into my office, I looked for anything that was amiss, especially dark attachments that could be draining, feeding on, or attacking them.

I was incredulous. Really?! The warrior shaman couldn't see a possession attached to himself? I was very sensitive to energy. If anything was around me, I could feel it. Plus, the souls around me—my protectors and counsel in the Realms—never alerted me. The numerous psychics I consulted with over the years did sense something, but they were vague, and since I couldn't see it, then for me, it just wasn't real.

Now that I knew, how would I disconnect from this possession, one that has been covertly attached to me for so long? I'd had energies attach to me before, but I could sense them. I didn't think this attachment was malicious. So, what then was its intent?

It seems to me predetermined.

Where in me is the fear? I need to sort what's mine and what's not.

I sense the boy. He is still attached to me. He doesn't have a body, yet I feel his energy overlain, like a second skin.

As the space between us widens, I can feel his fear as separate from mine. His fear and my fear are distinct. If an observer were witnessing this, it would look like two spheres bound to each other.

I speak with him. He tells me his name is Yakov.

I tell him it is time. He needs to go to the light.

I look up and all my soul helpers are there with me. In their protective way, they are ready to attack and crush this soul who dared hide himself so successfully within me.

These beings attack first and think later. I've experienced this so many times.

However, I am not called to attack. Rather, love and compassion take over.

I have a revelation: Yakov was killed in the camp. And then, I think he had drifted around until he was able to attach to me. Or maybe he was told to do so? By whom? What kind of beings have that kind of Power? I am curious to know more.

It is time to lead him to the light.

My soul helpers and I work as a team. We open up a space—a hole, of sorts, in the time-space continuum. Yakov is drawn in.

It happens quickly. He needs to go. I sense relief, too. He wants to go.

Yes, something seems destined to me about all this. I don't think Yakov had a choice to attach to me. I think we had a karmic connection that needed to play out.

There is no force or violence, only love and light. There is no darkness. This situation is atypical for me.

The Rebbe looks up and smiles at me. He is in a temple with many long tables where rabbis are praying and studying.

Two weeks later, I saw Ginnie. I asked, "Did you know of the soul that was attached to me?"

She looked directly at me. And then away. She started channeling:
The soul had always been there. In the camp you were very young, maybe eight or nine. I see you in knickers with stockings and an Irish type of hat. You radiate light. It is bright light that attracts all of the children in the camp. Hundreds of them.

Your job is to transmute the energy and send them to the light before you are all killed. You do not get that opportunity before you die. So the souls of the children are stuck in limbo.

Yakov is there. He attaches to you as a reminder about the camp.

His fear is an anchor so you won't forget the camp. When you got the gift, you could come back and finish the job. That is why they were all waiting for you to lead them.

In that life in the camp, you radiated bright light, like the rays from the sun. This is how you attracted all of the souls.

In other lives you had lots of darkness. In this life, you use both light and dark in balance.

I left Ginnie's office near central Massachusetts. By the time I got home—an hour later—she had sent me an email with additional descriptions and insight:

The light you radiated was as bright as the sun. You were a beacon. Each ray you sent out was a way for them to come to you, as the trauma of the times required assistance and you were sent to do this job of collecting men, women, and children.

The glee and joy you emanated upon arrival at the camp was exactly what the departing souls needed.

You collected one million traumatized men, women, and children. During the process of transmutation, one soul remained—as you were killed—to remind you what needed to be done in this lifetime.

Now I understood. This was extraordinary.

In the early 2000s, I was sitting in my office working with Joshua. I met him at the New England School of Acupuncture (NESA) when I was teaching a course there. He was an observant Jew. Uniquely, when we were together, he had visions relating to Judaism. Joshua often invited me to join him in his visions to figure out what was going on. This time was no exception.

Joshua said, "I have been having this vision. Would you please look at it for me?"

I enter his vision. I am in both ordinary and non-ordinary reality at once:

There is an old man, an ultra-orthodox Jew. We can tell because of the way he is clad. It looks like how the Hassids dressed circa 1700s in Poland. He is wearing an old-style black suit with a white shirt and black hat on his head. His beard is long and grey.

He doesn't move. His face is angular, chiseled, like a statue, with no expression.

I ask the old man, "Who are you?"

He replies, "I am the Amshinover Rebbe."

The old man appears behind Joshua, yet he seems as though he is standing there in a room with us.

Behind him are rows of tables in a large room. It looks like a Hassidic temple with many old Jews studying and praying.

I ask Joshua, "Do you know which Rebbe this is?"

I need clarification because the head Rebbe is always named after the town from which they came. The Rebbe tells me the name of the town, but neither Joshua nor I have heard of it.

Joshua has no idea what I am talking about. He can see what I see in the vision, but he can't hear the responses from the people I encounter.

There is Power here. The vision of the Rebbe is so clear, so real to me.

All the men continue studying. They are focused on their books, sometimes talking between themselves. I can't grasp what they are saying. None of them ever look up or acknowledge my presence.

Joshua asks, "What's going on, John?"

I say, "When I have visions, I don't hear words. A message comes directly to my mind, similar to dokusan in Zen practice, when I receive mind-to-mind transmissions."

I was curious to know which Rebbe I had encountered.

Together, Joshua and I did a Google search to find out. When he was alive, this Rebbe was a Tzadik, a spiritual leader of his community, the founder of an original branch of Hassidic ultra-orthodox Judaism. These branches—lineages—are usually named after the town where they lived. His branch is from a town in Russia.

For many years, in the Realms, this Rebbe would come to me. I had the same vision of the Hassidic temple with men studying and praying around long table. No one would acknowledge my presence. The Rebbe never spoke to me. He always looked directly at me, though. I had no idea what these encounters were about.

Was there a connection to me receiving the gift of Grace when I felt an enormous wave of compassion embrace me? I knew then, it was Grace—the word of God.

I needed to know more. In meditation, I encountered the Rebbe. He came to me, as I did not call upon him.

The Rebbe smiles at me. He has appeared in all my previous encounters over the years, but this time, it's different. The men at the tables look up and notice me. The Rebbe is clearly happy with what is happening.

Soon after, I met with Ginnie in her office.

I asked her, "How is the Rebbe connected to the story of the concentration camp?"

Ginnie is not Jewish. She knew nothing about ultra-orthodox ways. She immediately went into a trance and began to channel:

The Rebbe is one of the original seeds that God planted when he made the world. You are, too.

His job was to make sure you are okay, doing what you are supposed to be doing. He's watching over you.

The One knew the Holocaust would happen. It knew how many souls would need to be reborn. It would be too much for the world to handle. So, he prepared the world for this, many lifetimes ahead of the situation.

In your lifetime—before you were in the camp—you agreed to do what was needed. So, it was preordained that you would do this work in the camp at age fourteen because you were innocent then. You were light and not a warrior.

You would be reborn in this lifetime, to learn how to balance light and dark energies.

Later that day, Ginnie sent me an email of a direct channeling from the Rebbe:

Who am I?
   I am the Rebbe.
   I am dressed in a long robe.
   I have two long curly pieces of hair hanging down the sides of my face.
   I have a square block of wood on my forehead with a circle on it. It covers my third eye, so my ego is not tempted to speak for God but to merely lend voice to the Word. My left wrist is adorned with the antenna ring, so I may always be attuned.
   My beard is long. As I begin to speak my body rocks from the waves of energy pouring into me. I am surrounded by God's light mind for me to hear clearly.
   I AM. I am the original seeder of the 144,000 Earth pod souls. They will require thousands of years to grow in accordance with the divine so they can become enlightened to all potential through the feeling body. My job is only to tend the seed and make sure the original I AM presence is fortified and never becomes depleted, holding each line. I tenderly care for the seed while it makes its evolution

through each incarnation until it reaches its enlightened state and can hold the light of God completely. My energy comes from God.

Body as temple of Spirit. He has promised. "If you will open the door of consciousness, of your heart, I will enter and abide with you. This is the Law, the Way, the Life itself!"

This was heavy stuff. I didn't know what to make of it. Ginnie's descriptions were fascinating. She described elements of ultra-orthodox Hassidic principles and doctrine, something I didn't have much experience with. Ginnie described some of the classic look: the long hair is called a *payos*, the forehead blocks are called *tefillin*, the rocking motion when praying is called *davening*. Yes, I had Jewish ancestry. But my immediate family was not steeped in religiosity. However, I knew I came from a line of rabbis. My great, great grandfather was a rabbi. This was all a mystery to me.

A few years later, Joshua came into my office. He took out of his backpack a very small book. It was in Hebrew. I did not know any Hebrew.

Joshua opened the book. To him, I remained in my office chair. Yet, I stepped out of time and entered the Realms.

Power surges through me. The room radiates bright golden light. My body dissolves into the energetic burst. I am subsumed by the energy of the One, a direct link to the Universe.

I hear a prayer, the Sh'ma. It is one of the basic prayers in Judaism recited at every service: "Sh'ma Yisrael Adonai Eloheinu Adonai Echad." *(It translates to, "Here Oh Israel, The Lord our God, the Lord is One.")*

I know instantly there is One God, as the Jewish mystics have said. I realize, too, that we are all one.

Hebrew letters start flowing from me. They are emanating from my being. I can't read them, however.

It seems like I am witnessing the beginning of the Universe when it is being created by the letters.

In the Torah, God created the world by speaking words. Hebrew words and the letters contain mystical Power. They are direct connections of information and Power from God that can be used to channel healing energy.

I can feel the loving energy of the Rebbe around me. He is smiling. The old Jewish men sitting at the tables look at me. They, too, have loving energy and are smiling.

I receive a clear message: "You shall love God. You shall surrender to God. You shall walk humbly with your God." *I recognize this as a quote from the Torah, spoken by the prophet Micah.*

I later learned that the book Joshua brought in was a copy of the Sefer Yetzirah. This is a very old book, perhaps dating back to Abraham. It is part of the Jewish mystical Kabbalah that conveys in writing how the things of our Universe came into existence. I looked on my bookcase. I was surprised to find I had a copy of the book; however, I found it difficult to understand because the text, translated from Hebrew to English, is confounding and confusing. I believe it was written in code so that only certain people would be able to comprehend its hidden meaning.

The resonance of this experience and its Power would last for months to come.

After I met Baba in 2022, I thought again of the Rebbe. I had not seen him in a while. Rebbe was present right away but still not talking to me. For some reason, it came into my mind that he was waiting for me to say something. So, I smiled at him. I called on Baba. Surrendered and opened up to him with love.

The same thing happens to me with the Rebbe as when I call on Baba. This time the light is different. Except this time the light is different. It is powerful but not as golden and feels colder. I feel very clear. It is almost the opposite of Baba.

The Rebbe becomes very happy. He does not speak as such but delivers a very clear message in my head: I have become THE LIGHT. That is why he is there. To help me in this task or to watch over me.

I am a creature of light, and it is very important for me to realize that. I understand a little of this after experiencing Grace in the camp. However, I had not gone deep enough there.

He is very happy. Smiling, he gestures for me to follow him farther into the light. The light and energy are overwhelming. I realize I need to learn to surrender into it.

Time passed. The Rebbe was still with me. The light got stronger over time. The Power that came over me was focused, clear, and strong. This Power allowed me to focus on my seeing and knowing. I also realized that this was another dharma transmission. In his transmission, the Rebbe was extremely compassionate. This was the main difference between the two. Baba, all love. Rebbe, compassion. For me, compassion is a combination of love and empathy. It has the desire to help solve one's suffering. A lot like Zen.

Just as my first life koan was learning how to transmute the warrior into love and light, I instantly realized I had come to solve my second life koan—I found my purpose for being in the concentration camp.

It was all very nice. Baba was love. Rebbe was compassion. We had all the bases covered. However, two other souls kept coming back to me from the past. Since I was a teenager, I had been drawn to a famous rabbi called the Baal Shem Tov and his famous student, Dov Ber of Mezeritch. They lived in the early 1700s in Poland and are considered the founders of modern Hassidism.

The Baal Shem Tov, which means "Speaker of the Good Name," is a term for a holy man who wields the secret name of God. He was also a Jewish mystic and healer. His given name was Israel ben Eliezer. His central teachings were having direct connection to the divine through prayer and the mystical use of Hebrew words and letters. To me, the mystical use of Hebrew words and letters is Jewish shamanism.

I sit in meditation. I call on Baba and the Rebbe. They come instantly. I know they are there because of the very bright whitish-yellow light they bring with them. Like when you are in a dark room and go out into the bright noon sunlight.

As usual, we spend some time leading lost souls to the light. I open up a space in front of me. I do this by sitting in the love and light that radiate from Baba and the Rebbe. I let my peripheral vision expand out to the sides. This creates an opening.

The more I let go, surrender to the One, the more Power will be at my command. Though it seems to be an oxymoron, that is the way the Universe works. The ultimate Power in the Universe comes from the One. The more I can let go of my ego, the more Power I will have to work with. If I do not, I will be in the way of the free flow of Power.

I watch and see what comes into the opening. It can be souls, patients, or other beings.

Today, Rebbe comes into my vision very strongly. His Power is directing me to look beyond him. He directs me to follow his lineage back in time. It is like I am traveling in a tunnel with glass walls. I can only see colors on the walls as they zoom by me. I seem to be traveling back in time. I can sense this because I can feel more and more resistance in the tunnel. Usually, I do not travel into the past.

Suddenly, the resistance in the tunnel stops. I look around me and see a middle-aged man dressed in old-fashioned Polish clothes. Black suit, white shirt, big black hat, long beard.

I ask, "Who are you?"

He responds, "I am Dov Ber of Mezeritch."

I think to myself, 'Oh my God, I am in the presence of the Baal Shem Tov's head student.'

He continues, "We are expecting you. Please follow me."

I am so in awe. I follow him into another room. Sitting in a chair, behind a desk, I see the Baal Shem Tov.

I am totally overwhelmed. I never, ever expected to see either one of these two great rabbis. I have thought of them since I was a teenager, but they never came to me.

I look into the Baal Shem Tov's eyes. Immediately, we merge into one being. Sort of like how it is with Baba. But I have always felt Baba's presence in and around me. Now, I literally become the Baal Shem Tov. It seems like I am one with him for hours. Since we are outside of time, who knows how long it is.

Suddenly, I am back in my meditation room. I am vibrating with energy. Filled with light. I am not sure I am breathing. I just encountered two heroes from my childhood.

One of my colleagues, Paddy, lived in Santa Fe. I met him at a seminar on animal communication in 2005. He can talk with any animal and uses his psychic abilities to help people, too.

During one phone conversation in early 2024, Paddy asked me, "Are you okay?"

I replied: "What do you see?"

He answered, "It is not clear to me, but something is really bothering you."

"Okay," I said. "Let's look at it."

I entered the Realms:

I feel a pull of energy. I ride it like a wave. It takes me to a concentration camp. It is familiar. I think, I've been here before. Although, something is quite different.

KOAN 5: ECHOES IN THE REALMS

This is visceral. I am triggered by something. The past is informing me. I was passive then. I won't be now. Then I know.

I said, "It's the Middle East, the latest war between Hamas and Israel in 2024 . . . the immense loss of life on both sides . . . there isn't an easy solution to this kind of decades-long struggle . . . violence is not the answer."

I didn't recall anything else because I was so distraught. To me, the attack by Hamas and the murder of 1,400 people was a pogrom. In medieval Europe when things got difficult, the Jews were blamed and attacked in their ghettos. The nobility incited the peasants to burn and kill every Jew that could be found. This vilification continued throughout centuries and led to the Holocaust.

When I heard of the attack, I was angry, enraged, infuriated. And afraid. My warrior archetype was incited to lash out. I wanted to kill. I had not felt this way for decades. I thought I had healed this part of me. Yet here it was—again.

When I calmed down, I went inward. I knew I had to send love to the part of me that died in the Holocaust.

I was fully aware, violence begets violence. In a war, more anger, rage, and death are not the answer—ever.

The next day, I met with Ginnie. We didn't need to talk for her to know what was going on. When I had a block with psychic seeing, Ginnie saw for me. I interpreted what she perceived so I could understand and use the information to heal.

I told her: "I've been triggered. I have not been able to let it go. Ho'oponopono is not working. I am resisting, again."

The layers the of the concentration camp story that I'd held since I was a child were so complex and almost beyond comprehension. Yet it was all so real to me. It unfolded both in and out of the Realms:

I have troubling, unexplained memories. I died in a concentration camp. In the Realms, a Tzadik gifted me grace, love, and compassion.

Ginnie triggered me to return to the camp. Hundreds of souls were waiting. I was to send them to the light.

Cancer treatment triggered deeper memories—my body tattooed and the stark brick buildings. Gas chambers. Slaughter. Doom. Why didn't I fight? PTSD. I can't breathe.

How to clear this energy? The Rebbe returned. Still, why am I not healing? Jessica saw Yakov, a boy in the camp. He had attached to me when I was born as a reminder about the camp. I was a beacon, I was told, for one million traumatized men, women, and children.

Joshua channeled the Amshinover Rebbe, one of the original seeds God planted when he made the world. It was preordained that I would do this work in the camp because I was light and not a warrior.

Baba—guru and saint—was love. He connected me, profoundly, to the One.

Rebbe was compassion and my link to the Baal Shem Tov, Jewish mystic and healer. His student Dov Ber of Mezeritch took me to him. We merged.

I didn't have to tell Ginnie any of this—she knew. I remained angry. I still wanted to kill. I sat in the chair, across from her, in complete control of my emotions, yet holding extreme inner pain.

Ginnie listened and then entered a trance state.

She spoke: "I see the divine feminine."

I joined her in her vision:

We see an energetic group representing the divine feminine, known by many names such as Kuan Yin, Mother Mary, Shekhinah, Spider Woman, White Buffalo Calf Woman, Isis, Tara, Kali.

I was familiar. I'd used this divine feminine Power many times before to transmute the energy around me. Also, I used it with my patients to help them shift their rage into love.

Ginnie pointed to the treatment room. I made my way to the table and laid down on it. I closed my eyes as she began her work. As an energy healer, she used many techniques to move healing energy such as massage, Reiki, crystals, stones, prayers, and bells.

Then, I invoked the divine feminine to connect with me:

Her energy field reaches out to me.
   I gather up my rage.
   I pass it to her . . . flowing from me to her.
   She immediately transmutes my rage into love.
   The love flows back to me.
   This comforts me.

I returned home.

The rage returned, on occasion. Yet, I realized I found another Way to stay in a place of love—for now.

I call Baba, Rebbe, Dov, and the Baal Shem Tov.
   They come.
   Often, one of them takes charge, or we all sit in the light together.
   This time, Baba leads.
   I feel overcome with bliss.
   The ecstasy is so powerful.
   The intensity overwhelms me.

This is extreme yang.
I respond with energy to counterbalance.
Then, I feel pain, loss, and grief.
The pain, too, is powerful.
The intensity overwhelms me.
This is extreme yin.
These feelings are strong.
I cannot remain in this space of extremes and dissonance.
I ask:
"Where is the balance?
"Where is Buddha's middle path?
"How do I find peace within this experience of yin and yang?
"How do I reconcile these energies?"
I quiet the bliss.
I quiet the grief.
By feeding each of them less Power.
Then, I feel an energetic shift.
I move past the extreme emotions and into yet another realm.
I am now in a place of the void, with darkness all around me.
In my mind, I hear the ending of the Heart Sutra in Sanskrit:

Gaté,
gaté,
paragaté,
parasamgaté.
Bodhi!
Svaha!

Gone,
gone,

gone beyond,
gone fully beyond.
Wisdom!
Awakened!

3:00 a.m. I began my meditation.

I call on Baba and Rebbe. They both are present instantly—Baba with his pure love and Rebbe with his infinite compassion. I have been trying to let go of the agony of the concentration camp. I've come to know this situation thoroughly with its terrifying, gruesome details. Recently, everything seems to trigger the intense memories and stirring emotions—especially fear and rage. The warrior in me is furious and wants to go berserk and kill.

I know I am standing in my own way. Why can't I release it? What am I missing? Both Baba and Rebbe hold me in their Power. They point to a path of light extending up and away from them.

I heed their direction and follow it. Then, I am carried by the light into a void where I connect to the One, where there is nothing and everything at the same time.

I hear a voice in my head. It clearly speaks: "I gave you the power of Grace years ago when you first came to the concentration camp. You have used it many times for many people. Why have you not used it for yourself?"

Then I know exactly what I need to do to heal myself.
When I turn, the camp appears instantly.

> *Rebbe is waiting for me, the same Rebbe who had gifted me Grace many years ago.*
>
> *This is an echo of my first encounter with him. This time, I know what to do.*
>
> *I sit in the power of Grace, the energy of the One. I let it in. It permeates my being. The Grace is warm, loving—beyond loving. I dissolve into the bliss. Nirvana.*
>
> *The connection fades as I come back to the present and return to my meditation room.*

This time, the pain of the camp did not return with me.

I let it go.

... again.

I thought: *It feels resolved.*

I am at peace.

... for now.

It was spring. Mike, John, and I had met to spar. It was cold and rainy, too wet to be outside. We didn't want the steel to get wet and rust. I took the cars out of the garage to make room for us to work inside. There was plenty of space for us to move around. The ceilings are ten feet high, which accommodates the movement of my five-and-half-foot long sword.

In between sparring, Mike and John asked me some questions. This time, I was not fully in the present, because I was slipping in and out of the Realms.

When I hold my sword, it transports me. My energy shifts. I become the mix of the archetypes I have carried in this lifetime—warrior, shaman, mystic, and healer. They merge.

Today the guys seemed especially talkative. Admittedly I don't recall what they were asking me, because I felt labelled. But Mike later recounted to me his barrage of questions: "Who did you study with?" "Who did you learn the most from?" "Does it matter if you learn from your teachers in person or in the Realms?" "Who was your favorite teacher?" "What specifically did you learn by teaching yourself?" Those questions focused on my life's work, of how I crafted a martial arts system that is non-violent and spiritual. This made me feel like I'm their guru. I don't feel comfortable with that. I don't see it that way. I'm no different than they are. I'm just called to follow my path. It's my Way, as a mystic who strives to connect to the One. The more I felt grilled, the deeper I moved into the Realms... until I disappeared.

Earlier I felt—no, I knew—something unusual was going to happen. That morning, during my meditation at 3:00 a.m., I had a profound connection with both Baba and Rebbe. Our energies had merged. I savored the serenity of the moment, of nothing to do, no shamanic workings, no one to save. This was my time. I dissolved into this timeless oneness, lasting many hours.

Later that morning, at 9:00 a.m. we were sparring in two rounds.

With John:

The movement of my steps builds the energy and yields a hypnotic-like trance. I do this, over and over, back and forth. My mind is actively engaged in the sparring yet boosted to receive any communication or download of ethereal knowledge.

I am wholly in the Realms.
I merge with the sword.
I see.
I feel.
I am the energy.
I know.
I let go.
I allow.
This is one expression of my Power.
This is me in my Power.
This is me as Power.

With Mike, I slowed the movements down.

A beautiful blue, white, and golden light emanates all around me.

I feel the condensed energy, the Power pulling him to me, even though he had just stepped back, away from me. He is caught in my vortex, like a tractor beam.

I dissolve into the consuming darkness.

The sword and I are one. We have merged. From Sword to No Sword. From here to nowhere. For that moment, and for some undefined length of time, I am invisible.

I am shapeshifting. I am soaring like a bird of prey. I am Brother Hawk.

My trance state, once expansive and radiating outward, intensifies as it condenses inward. Now infused with this energy, I intentionally draw Power into me.

Both Baba and Rebbe appear.

I was surprised. Often, when I enter the Realms while sparring I encounter historical and mythological martial artists. Today, it was unusual for my spiritual teachers to appear.

Baba on my left. Rebbe on my right. They direct me to look up.

Suddenly, there is a bright white light extending downward toward me, like a tube. The light envelopes me, permeates my whole body, and anchors deep into the earth.

Then I am drawn upwards. My body dissolves. The Sword disappears.

My body and mind disperse as I alchemically join ... with the One.

I had connected with the One many times before. I have had many satori experiences over the years. I have had a few full enlightenment experiences, too. However, nothing like this.

I am in a state of indescribable bliss.
Nothing else exists.
A beautiful blue, white, and gold light emanates all around me.

At some time, I had let go of the sword. Mike had taken it from me so it wouldn't fall to the floor. John steadied me. They led me to a chair, sat me in it and waited for my consciousness to return.

This was my mountain. I scaled it. This journey was complete. Baba helped me solve my first life koan: I integrated my warrior, shaman, mystic, and healer archetypes. Rebbe helped me solve the second life koan: understanding my role in the Holocaust concentration camp saga. To my surprise, the sword was the impetus and channel for Grace. In other lives I experienced so much darkness. I was out of balance. In this life, I learned to use both light and dark as complementary energies. This is yin/yang. Neither exists without the other. The darkness and light are now in harmony. Also, I discovered Grace as an expression of the One. My teachers echoed these lessons for me in the Realms. Baba with love. Rebbe with compassion.

I enter the Realms for solace, guidance and healing.
I reach a place of peace, presence, and connection.
I have never felt this level of consciousness before.
. . . enveloped by the aura of the One.
I unite with the One.
I Am.
Home.

QUESTIONS FOR SELF-REFLECTION

- Where do your deep sorrows live or hide?

- How can you transmute your sorrow through loving energy?

- How can you use that energy as Power?

- How could you use this transformed Power in service to the One?

Afterword

When reviewing my life story, I now clearly see my growth and progression—an evolution from a warrior to a healer, from darkness to light.

It seems my life has been a test. *Can I pull it off?* I sometimes wondered. Each of the stories I have written about has changed me. Zen. Calling the Souls. Sword. Threshold Guardian. The Realms. Thematically, each chapter chronicles my life journey.

I hadn't anticipated the contents of this book would jar my memory and profoundly stir my emotions. Recounting so many anecdotes was a deep dive into some extraordinary moments of joy and stinging pain, too, some of which distressed me to recall.

My life has not been linear. There were many twists and turns. I suppose any memoir evokes a sense of wistful nostalgia and musing: *Is all of this a dream?* Surely not. It all happened over the span of some seventy years. Ultimately, it was a journey to the One.

In hindsight, I am awed by the time and energy I devoted to connecting in the Realms. That is the way of a shaman, a title I evaded for decades. Yet, as a mystic and spirit walker in service to those who entrust me with their suffering, I must concede to my inexplicable commitment, like a moth drawn to the flame. I return to the Realms, daily, in service to myself and those in need.

Why? Because:

The Realms call me.
    The Realms inform me.
    The Realms embrace me.
    The Realms challenge me.
    The Realms both comfort and confound me.
    The Realms hone me.
    The Realms are timeless, a fluid continuum of time and space.
    I traverse the Realms.
    I find my way seamlessly from here to there, to non-ordinary reality and back.
    Yes, the Realms are ethereal—yet they overlap with and cast shadows on my earthly plane existence.
    Power is there—born, propagated, and recycled in the Realms—for me to bask in, to cultivate, to access, to absorb, to channel, and to direct.
    In the Realms are moments, minutes, hours. Connected to Source. Communing with facets of the One. Completely entranced, ceding my essence in quantum entanglement.
    In the Realms, every time is different and yet the same. It is Zen. Each moment guides me—mostly to be, sometimes to witness or engage.
    In the Realms, I am both visitor and denizen, discovering, often growing, and progressing.
    It seems dreamlike, at times. Yet it is always grounded in either stark or wondrous realities.

The work for me will continue throughout my remaining time on this Earth. Mindful of Zen. Calling the Souls. Wielding the

Sword (and No Sword). Challenging Threshold Guardians. Traversing the Realms. Blessed with Grace.

My path—*my* Way—is of the Red Dragon. I am the Red Dragon, known through Inner Alchemy, Shamanic Power, and the Journey Within.

OTHER BOOKS BY JOHN MYERSON

Riding the Spirit Wind: Stories of Shamanic Healing. John Myerson with Jay Thomas. Second Edition. 2025.

Death Grip on the Pommel: A Warrior's Journey to Grace. John Myerson & Judith Robbins. 2011.

Voices from the Other Side of the Couch: A Warrior's View of Shamanic Healing. John Myerson & Judith Robbins. 2008.

For more information and other resources, visit our website at WayoftheRedDragon.com.

Or email us at info@wayofthereddragon.com.

About the Authors

John G. Myerson, Ph.D., Lic. Ac. is a graduate of Harvard College and the first class of the New England School of Acupuncture. He received his doctorate in psychology from the Union Institute & University. John practices shamanic healing, Oriental medicine and psychotherapy. He is one of the founders of the New England School of Acupuncture and was its first President. For almost sixty years he has studied, practiced, and taught Zen, yoga, Taoist cultivation, martial arts, and shamanic practices. He lives on a horse farm outside of Boston with his wife of over fifty years, four dogs, and eighteen horses.

Jay Thomas, M.A., M.Ed. is a health/wellness coach and shamanic practitioner. He leads workshops and retreats throughout New England. Jay trained in Harner Shamanic Counseling through the Foundation for Shamanic Studies. He is a board member and presenter for the Society for Shamanic Practices, Northeast Chapter. His complementary training and experience include tarot, body/mind studies, insight and mindfulness meditation, Usui Reiki and Shamballa Multidimensional Healing, Wicca and Ceremonial Magick, and mediumship. Jay has worked with John Myerson since 2009. He lives in Western Massachusetts at the base of a small mountain—across a river, down a dirt road, beside a stream, nestled in the forest.

www.ingramcontent.com/pod-product-compliance
Lightning Source LLC
Chambersburg PA
CBHW070528010526
44110CB00049B/1302